ROCK 'N' ROLL CaMP FOR GiRLS

RNRC4G !

Camp for Girls

how to
Start A Band, Write Songs, Record an Album, and ROCK OUT!!

Edited by MARISA ANDERSON
Foreword by CARRIE BROWNSTEIN
of Sleater-Kinney

CHRONICLE BOOKS
SAN FRANCISCO

Library of Congress Cataloging-in-Publication Data:

Rock 'n' roll camp for girls : how to start a band, write songs, record an album, and rock out! / edited by
    Marisa Anderson ; foreword by Carrie Brownstein of Sleater-Kinney.
        p. cm.
    ISBN 978-0-8118-5222-7
    1. Rock groups—Vocational guidance—Juvenile literature. 2. Rock music—Instruction and study—Juvenile. 3. Women rock musicians—Vocational guidance—Juvenile literature. 4. Rock 'n' Roll Camp
    for Girls (Portland Or.)—Juvenile literature. I. Anderson, Marisa.

    ML3795.R643 2008
    781.660835'2—dc22

                    2008010677

Manufactured in Canada

Designed by JACOB T. GARDNER
Photographs by SHAYLA HASON
Illustrations by NICOLE GEORGES on pages 1, 2–3, 16–17, 33, 34–35, 43, 55, 59, 72–73, 77, 79,
        86–87, 90, 93, 109, 110, 112–113, 127, 143, 147, 148–149, 151, and 157; sts on pages 61,
        99, 129, and 140; MARISA ANDERSON on pages 71 and 98; AMANDA PAULK on pages 89 and
        103; and JODI DARBY on page 141.
Typeset in ITC Franklin Gothic, Helvetica Neue, ITC American Typewriter, FRANKFURTER
        HIGHLIGHT and LazyBones ET

10 9 8 7 6 5 4 3 2 1

Chronicle Books LLC
680 Second Street
San Francisco, CA 94107
www.chroniclebooks.com

Table of Contents

Foreword

Everything at the Rock 'n' Roll Camp for Girls takes place in a single week. For anyone out there who's ever tried to write a song, start and finish a painting, or make a film, you know one week is nothing. One week is the time it takes for an adult to *think* about what we have to do: prepare and procrastinate, produce a draft, doubt we are capable, fail, and start again. But one week is all it takes for young girls, some of whom have never strummed a guitar chord in their life, held drum sticks in their hands, or stepped foot on a stage, to come together with complete strangers, form a band, and write a song that will blow your mind.

These girls are between the ages of eight and eighteen. They come from all regions of the United States; they travel from Europe, Asia, and Australia. Or they come from the neighborhoods of Portland, Oregon, where the camp is located. Some choose Rock Camp over horse camp, soccer camp, and theater camp; some have never been to camp or have never had the opportunity to go. Maybe they've taken a few piano or guitar lessons, maybe their older brother or dad played in a band,

maybe their parents have a great record collection, or maybe they thought music was something only other people made. They are nerds, cheerleaders, cool kids, weirdos, budding intellectuals—some on the edge of failing, or maybe not sure who they are. Because rock music has become so watered down and homogenized, we forget that music is still a medium for social change and personal transformation. Rock music was once about breaking rules, but in this day and age, skintight jeans and leather jackets mean nothing and break no rules at all. If you want to break the rules, you create a place for the most unlikely people—who look nothing like the music icons we see in magazines—to not just break rules, but to invent new ones.

Maybe it's watching the invention of new rules that makes grown men cry. I've seen a father cry at every Rock Camp showcase I've been to. I've seen men cry who don't have a daughter at Camp, who merely showed up to watch a dozen or so brand-new bands strut their stuff. They cry and I cry, because we are so rarely surprised anymore. And to be surprised, to truly be caught off guard, by something so unself-conscious, is to realize that a lot of what we believe to be bold is really quite tame. Bold is not a wanky guitar solo at Madison Square Garden that lasts five minutes while hundreds of thousands of dollars' worth of lights and pyrotechnics tell an audience when to applaud. Nor is bold a bassist jumping from the top of the kick drum and doing a scissor kick in the air at the end of a song. Bold is learning how to play the drums on Monday and performing in front of five hundred people on Saturday. Bold is screaming into a microphone, or merely talking into one, when you didn't even know you could. Bold makes the hair stand up on the listeners' necks, gives them a lump in the back of their throat, makes them happy to be alive.

This is the part where I should talk about the importance of the words "for Girls" in the name of the Rock Camp. The next time you pick up a music magazine's "Best of" issue and see maybe one woman listed, if any, you'll know why the Camp is for girls. There have always been women playing music. Just because you can't name more than a handful doesn't mean they never existed. Sometimes the greatest players—and great moments, melodies, vocal lines, note bends, snare hits, stumbles and regains—go unnoticed the first time around, or maybe they never get noticed. It's the audience's job to pay attention, to seek out the undiscovered and unsung, but a musician's sense of self-worth can't rely on the audience. So, Camp is about self-discovery. It's more important to take notice of yourself and of your own capabilities than it is for other people to take notice. Luckily, people are noticing. It's hard not to.

One thing the campers learn at Rock Camp is to be unafraid. And to be unafraid you have to know what you're doing, at least a little bit. Technical jargon can seem

like a secret, and Rock Camp cracks the code. You learn the language, the lingo, how to demystify the complex gadgetry and gear. It's hard to ask for things—not knowing renders you powerless. But at Camp, you discover that it's safe to ask, and asking makes you powerful. You learn what to ask for in a monitor mix, how to tune, what your amp and pedal settings should be, what is causing the floor tom to ring out. Camp lets you practice your windmills, jumps, and other stage moves. Rock Camp is a series of secret handshakes—it gives you all of the information you need to know.

Rock camp isn't music camp. The campers are not just learning technique as much as they are learning how to communicate in a way that they aren't usually allowed to. Not many mediums applaud the unhinged, the heartbroken, the moments of imbalance followed by ones of steadiness—but rock does. When girls are allowed to let go and not be called crazy, or to yell without being called angry, then they learn that the world they live in is limitless—or at least that the possibilities are. Girls discover that they draw their own boundaries, that they can push those boundaries through art, that they can be heard. And you don't have to yell; you can stand onstage and sing the prettiest, quietest song, commanding an entire room with your voice. To reach the back of the room and beyond with a sound you create, that will change your world. You have to be able to imagine that you are bigger than you are, especially when girls are usually taught to be smaller, both literally and figuratively. It all comes back to making a sound, making a noise. If you are lucky enough to hear it, you will be moved. If you are even luckier and you get to make the sound, you will forever be changed.

It's easy to become intimidated or cynical and forget about the reasons why people set out to create. We forget that most musicians or bands (at least the great ones) started playing because of a natural attraction or sense of urgency or out of raw necessity. In basement or practice space or living room, whatever the provenance, there has yet to be judgment from the outside and everything is still undefined. I hope this book will bring that galvanizing space into the home of any girl who gets her hands on it.

When as many as twenty bands get on stage at the Rock Camp Showcases, they play because they have to and because they want to, even though they may never see each other again. They are not thinking about tomorrow, or who will review the show, or if anyone is listening or understanding. They're not even thinking about the moment, because they're in the moment, and it's fleeting, so they better make the best of it. And they're thinking about the sound, how it's bigger than they are, bigger than Camp, bigger than all of the forces that will conspire against them, and they

than Camp, bigger than all of the forces that will conspire against them, and they know that for that moment they own the sound: It is theirs. Hopefully, if you give a young girl this moment and this sound, she'll tell the world, and the world will listen.

— Carrie Brownstein, Sleater-Kinney
Portland, Oregon

introductioN

This book is for anybody who ever dreamed of playing music. It is for girls who have been to the Rock 'n' Roll Camp for Girls and girls who have never heard of the Camp; for women who say, "I wish there had been something like Rock Camp when I was a kid"; and for men who've played in bands for years and have daughters who love music. We are delighted to realize that first-year Rock campers were born into a world that contains a place just for them; our dream is that these girls will never have to play alone.

The information and inspiration contained within these pages represents the collective wisdom of women who work hard at their craft, play from their hearts, and have the common sense to know that sharing their knowledge and experience benefits us all. These are women who want to help the next generation of girls succeed bravely at whatever they are inspired to try; who know that Rock Camp is not only about music—it's about taking risks and being supported, it's about community and the strength that is gained by knowing you are not alone in the world.

The following essays, photos, and drawings were created with love by just a fraction of the hundreds of staff, volunteers, and Rock campers who make up this far-flung community of music lovers, activists, musicians, girls, and women (and a few men) who have poured their hearts and souls into realizing the potential in every girl who walks through the doors of the warehouse we call home.

Each of the contributors was chosen, or chose themselves, in an open call to the Rock Camp community. The goal was to represent in print the breadth and diversity of

topics covered during a week at Camp. Some of these essays just scratch the surface of their topic, hopefully inspiring further research, while other essays illuminate topics that have not been covered in the mainstream media.

From instrument instruction to self-defense, each of the essays in this book can be used as a doorway to self-discovery. Maybe you'll find out that the inner workings of a sound system are totally fascinating, or maybe you'll be encouraged to start an all-ages club in your hometown. Who knows, maybe you'll even start a new Rock Camp!

Rock Camp is about saying YES to the creative possibilities within every girl. Our hope is that we have produced a book you will return to again and again, whether reading every word straight through, researching the answer to a particular question, or opening it up at random to learn something new and inspiring on your way to uncovering your own creative possibilities.

Marisa Anderson
artistic director, Rock 'n' Roll Camp for Girls
Portland, Oregon

tO EVERYONE WHO READS THiS BOOk

When the Rock 'n' Roll Camp for Girls Summer Camp began in Portland, Oregon, in 2001, it didn't take long for word to spread to musicians on the East Coast. Over the course of the first few summers of the camp's existence, women musicians started making the pilgrimage from New York, Boston, and other eastern towns and cities out to Portland, in greater numbers every year, to take part in the unbelievable experience of Rock Camp.

I first heard about it on the radio. I think I was eating dinner and only half listening to the story, but once I got the gist of what the camp was about, I had the classic drop-your-fork, drop-your-jaw response.

I was (and am) a musician and songwriter, a feminist, and a fan of new adventures. I really wanted to go to Rock Camp. So I filled out a volunteer application, signed up to teach bass, and bought a plane ticket. That was the summer of 2003. I went back in 2004.

Each time, I came home overflowing with stories about the camper bands, the workshops, the showcase concert at the end of camp . . . gushing like I was in love. Which I was: I was wowed by everything I had witnessed and participated in. I felt excited about the revolutionary possibilities of encouraging girls to get loud and experience their own power, and to cheer on other girls and women, all through the vehicle of music. And working with the camper bands made me feel rejuvenated about my own music—"Writing a song and then playing it? How amazing!"

Back home, it seemed illogical and unacceptable to me that New York didn't have a rock camp of its own, and incredibly urgent that someone get one up and running

as quickly as possible. I wasn't alone in feeling this way. Some of my fellow New York musicians who had volunteered at the camp in Portland were eager to get involved, and we started recruiting our friends, and so on. . . .

We decided to name our camp the Willie Mae Rock Camp for Girls, in honor of Willie Mae "Big Mama" Thornton, the guitarist, singer, and songwriter who wrote "Ball and Chain" and who was the first artist to record "Hound Dog." Over the course of a full year of planning, the ideas kept coming, new supporters signed on, we got our first grant, found a place to do our first camp session, and the camper and volunteer applications started rolling in. The next thing we knew, IT WAS TIME TO ROCK AND ROLL.

At our inaugural session, held in August 2005, we had sixty-six campers, and about as many volunteers. It was a messy, beautiful, cacophonous week, culminating in a joyous showcase concert. We were all—organizers, volunteers, campers, and parents alike—completely hooked. We've grown a lot since then, and every summer is filled with new adventures.

To everyone who reads this book: We hope to inspire you to seek out new adventures. We hope you feel encouraged to write your first song, or your hundred-and-first one; to start a band; to play or sing "wrong" notes and "right" notes and beats and chords that you invented yourself; to open your ears and your minds to new sounds; to ask any and all questions, big or small; and to believe in your own power to SHAKE IT UP.

Karla Schickele
director, Willie Mae Rock Camp for Girls
New York, New York

Where We've Been

How did Rock Camp start? Why is it necessary? What stories can be told by the girls who have come before us, and why is it important to stay true to yourself in the pursuit of your musical dreams? The answers to these questions help us to define who we are and where we're going, as individuals and as a community of musicians and music lovers.

The story of Rock Camp must be told as just a part of the larger story of the roles girls and women have played in the music industry and how those roles have changed over time. Today, more than ever, women have the power to choose who they work with, what they sound like, and how they want to put their music and their image out into the world. For girls interested in playing music, it's important to know that there are as many paths to musical success as there are ideas of what success is.

LEt There be ROCK

BY STS

POWER

VOLUME   REVOLUTION

ROCK'N'ROLL
CAMP FOR GIRLS
PORTLAND, OREGON

ROCK-N-ROLL
GIRLS CAMP TIX
ARE
SOLD OUT!

THE STORY OF THE ROCK 'N' ROLL CAMP FOR GIRLS BEGINS with a statistic and some troubling research. In the year 2000, Janis Joplin was the first female artist mentioned on VH1's *100 Greatest Artists of Hard Rock*. Janis broke into the list at number 48, followed by five other female artists. Six women, surrounded by ninety-four male artists.

This fact, juxtaposed with research showing that girls who start school scoring ahead of boys often leave school scoring behind them, and that this decline in girls' performance can be directly linked to a slide in self-esteem,[1] was cause for alarm for many, and spurred some to action, including the soon-to-be founders of the Rock 'n' Roll Camp for Girls.

Rock Camp was started by women who believed that they could create a program using music education to enhance self-esteem and develop life skills in girls. Rock Camp founder Misty McElroy developed the initial weeklong day camp as her Senior Capstone Project, a community service graduation requirement for Portland State University seniors.

McElroy and several volunteers, including Patti Duncan of the PSU Women's Studies Department, set out to incorporate music education, creation, and performance as a means of building self-esteem and fostering confidence in girls and young women. Rock Camp was created as a place for girls to learn, explore, and create music in a supportive environment. Without the self-esteem and life skills components, the Rock 'n' Roll Camp for Girls would be just another music camp.

Community support for the fledgling camp blasted expectations. Parent interest was piqued as this fantastic concept hit the front page of the *Portland Tribune*. Camper enrollment, at $25 per girl, skyrocketed beyond the camp's capacity. Volunteer instructors, counselors, coaches, and workshop leaders packed the volunteer training and demolished every slice of pizza set out for lunch.

The 2001 Showcase Concert immediately sold out, with barely enough room for a hundred campers, their cheering family members, and volunteers. Bass players who had never seen their instrument before Monday boomed their way on Saturday night through bass lines they had learned in a week. Ten-year-old girls proudly showed off their new beats, power chords, vocal harmonies, and innovativeness: One group, called the Hot Jumps, styled their drumbeats to accompany their jump-rope skills.

From the beginning, Rock Camp's mission was to teach music to girls, but programming didn't stop there. To this day, every instrument instruction class, band practice, and workshop is taught, coached, or led by a girl or woman with experience in her field.

Campers arrive at 9 A.M. each morning and go home at 5 P.M., having spent a full day immersed in band practice, instrument instruction, and workshops in subjects like zine writing, where they learn the power of self-expression through self-publication. Girls attend lyric-writing workshops led by experienced female

1 - NYU Child Study Center online, Anita Gurian, Ph.D. "Gifted Girls—Many Gifted Girls, Few Eminent Women: Why?" http://www.aboutourkids.org/articles/gifted_girls_many_gifted_girls_few_eminent_women_why (accessed December 14, 2007).

musicians who share tricks and tips for getting words on paper. Another workshop, self-defense, introduces the concept that girls can and should protect themselves physically, emotionally, and mentally. These workshops tie together the importance of a strong sense of self-worth and the development of life skills with learning an instrument, playing in a band, and writing a song in a genre of music that historically has said "no girls allowed."

Originally intended as a one-time-only event, Rock Camp captivated an entire community. A group of Portland's businesspeople, musicians, child educators and advocates, feminists, and parents stepped up and helped secure the future of the Rock 'n' Roll Camp for Girls.

In 2002, the Native American Youth Association (NAYA) graciously donated their building in North Portland for the week. The relatively small ballroom housed 125 students and more than 100 volunteers. Band practice was annexed out to a pizza parlor down the street. The guitar class took up the entire upper floor of the building, while six drum sets crowded into a single room downstairs. Self-Care workshops were scheduled between Sound and Lighting. Panelists from women-owned independent record labels doubled as instructors and counselors. More kids wanted to come, more volunteers wanted to get involved, and the second Rock 'n' Roll Camp for Girls Showcase was held at the Aladdin Theater, tripling the capacity of the previous year's venue. Once again, it sold out.

In the beginning of 2003, Rock Camp moved to its current location in an old industrial sewing factory located on the northern edge of town. Here, among the sounds of a neighboring machine shop and the Columbia Slough, bands can practice and eight-year-olds can bang on drums. The parking lot that stretches along a

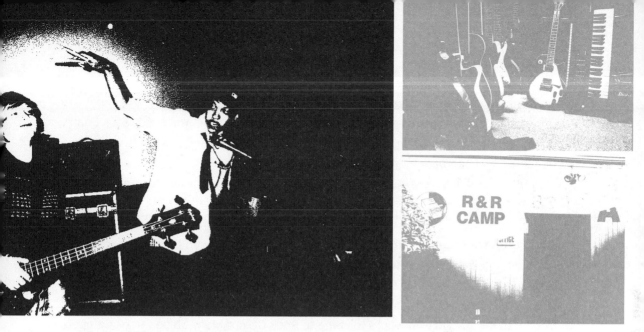

small stand of birch trees holds four portable toilets as well as the parked cars of volunteers. Two picnic tables placed at the edge of the trees provide a small respite from the heat generated by 150-plus bodies.

Our beloved warehouse holds the necessary electric power for thirty amps to plug in and crank up, and space for thirteen practice rooms. There is also a large, well-lighted community space in the far back, dubbed the Rock Room. The Rock Room serves as the lunchroom and large group workshop space, where campers can eat while watching live rock shows, women DJs spinning, or hip-hop artists at work. During Summer Camp sessions, every room is crowded with instruments, cables, drum sets, musicians, and volunteers. Summer Camp is a sweaty, riotous party with hours and hours of punk, rock, and pop stacked on top of each other.

In the fall of 2003, the Rock Camp year-round program, called the Girls Rock Institute (GRI), opened its doors. Rock Block, the primary after-school program, gives local Portland female musicians a chance to work with girls in an ongoing, sustained relationship. Rock Block is a two-hour class for girls ages eight to eighteen. The first hour consists of beginner, intermediate, and advanced instruction on guitar, bass, drums, keyboards, or vocals. During the second hour, bands create an original song, working each session to write, develop, and practice it for the end-of-term Showcase Concert.

Bands that form at Rock Block may stay together for ten weeks, or a whole year. They can get help from a band coach to book shows and record their songs. Operating year-round, GRI has grown to offer instrument instruction, band formation,

band practice, workshops, private lessons, and band coaching to hundreds of girls in Portland and the surrounding areas.

Students ages sixteen to eighteen with extended Summer Camp and GRI experience can choose to work as interns and serve on the Youth Advisory Board. Many of the volunteers at Summer Camp and some Rock Block staff were once students and campers themselves!

Starting in April 2004, Ladies Rock Camp arrived in answer to the frequently asked question: "Why didn't this camp exist when I was a girl?" In the course of three days, fifty women campers convene to form bands, learn their instruments, and perform a show. Wishing to provide the adult campers with the same experience as their younger counterparts, band formation, instrument instruction, workshops, and most of the schedule mimics Summer Camp. With sessions three times a year, Ladies Rock Camp currently generates enough funds to support financial-aid requests for any girl who wants to come to Rock Camp. Many Ladies Rock Campers are inspired by their daughters, nieces, friends, and little sisters who attend Summer Camp or GRI. Imagine your mom or grandma playing the guitar or singing in a rock band. It happens at the Ladies Rock Camp Showcase!

In 2005, documentary filmmakers Arne Johnson and Shane King came to Rock Camp to follow four campers and tell their stories in the feature film *Girls Rock! The Movie* (released in March 2008). The movie shows the ups and downs of conflict and resolution within a band, the challenges of writing a song on the same day as learning to play an instrument, and the excitement of learning to get along with seventy-five new best friends. In spite of the potentially intimidating presence of the filmmakers, the girls were by no means passive subjects, as Arne and Shane soon learned. When the campers discovered that one of the directors had left the toilet seat up, they retaliated with a bold stroke of graffiti: "Put the seat down! YR on grrrl turf!" To this day, the scrawl is there for all our visiting boys to see when they lift the seat. Over time, this funny and awkward moment turned into our biggest shared joke with the directors, who have since used *Girls Rock!* to promote and support Rock Camp as much as possible.

In 2007, with incredible support from our community of parents, students, campers, musicians, and foundations, the Rock 'n' Roll Camp for Girls reached out to several like-minded programs to form the Girls Rock Camp Alliance. The GRCA is an association of Girls Rock Camps from around the world who share in common the mission of building self-esteem and leadership skills in girls through music education and performance. GRCA members attend yearly conferences to network and support

new organizations modeled after the Rock 'n' Roll Camp for Girls. As new Girls Rock Camp–style organizations spread all over the world, the GRCA provides a central resource to help parents, campers, and volunteers locate Rock Camps that are committed to teaching girls how to play instruments and form bands in a supportive environment.

In 2007, we also added 16 Records, an on-site volunteer- and intern-run record label and distributor; a year-round intern program; and the Youth Advisory Board. In 2007, Hip Hop Elements began at Summer Camp and has now joined GRI with two-hour classes every week where students can learn break dancing, DJing, beat making, and MCing.

Programs and workshops are constantly evolving, but Rock Camp's mission to build girls' self-esteem through music creation and performance still stands as the strength and binding force behind everything we do. And everything we will do for years to come.

ReAL GiRLS ROCK

BY SARAH DOUGHER

When you think about girls playing rock music, who do you think of? Hanna Montana? Britney Spears on *The Mickey Mouse Club*? Maybe you think about you and your friends playing music in your room. You may think of famous people, or people who aren't so famous. But one thing is certain: as long as rock 'n' roll has been around, girls have been playing music together and totally rocking. You may not have heard of very many of them, but they are there.

By "girls," I mean people who started or experienced a big part of their music career before they were twenty years old. Since the 1960s, girls and women have been working in the music industry in more visible ways than ever before, and today there are still more opportunities for young women to make their mark in the world of music. But even before the women's liberation movement of the late '60s, girls and women were playing music together, helping each other out, and making their presence felt in a world dominated by men. Have you heard of the Carter Family?

What about Carla Thomas? Clara Ward? The Ronettes? The Shangri-Las? These and so many more girls paved the way for innovations in music that we still feel today. They also endure as great role models in the music industry.

In the public eye, girls are often stereotyped in ways that make them seem weak. This is true in most books about the annals of rock 'n' roll, which almost never include any information about girls and their contributions to this important history.

One common stereotype is when historians talk about girls as FANS of music. The images of the screaming girls who greeted the Beatles are as important as the images of the Beatles themselves—really, we couldn't have one without the other. But it makes girls look crazy and out of control if this is the only image we see.

Another image we see is girls buying records as CONSUMERS. Girls in this role are able to buy and watch and listen to music, but they don't make it. These stereotypes are limiting, especially since girls are not the only people who are fans and consumers. We all play those roles at certain times, whether we are girls or boys, women or men. Even if the history books haven't caught up yet, it is pretty obvious that girls and women are writing, playing, producing, and performing—*creating!*—music.

When rock 'n' roll first emerged in popular culture, girls were right there. Their contributions span the whole history of rock, including some styles of music that are at the roots of rock 'n' roll. Blues, country and western, **R&B**, rockabilly, and gospel are all forms of music that came together to make rock 'n' roll, and female artists had a huge impact on the evolution of all these styles of music. I've selected four artists who I think played an important part in the way rock developed in the United States. They all sound very different, but they each tell an interesting story about what it was like to be a girl playing music during their era.

First, I want to introduce you to Janis Martin, who was a leading rockabilly singer when she was only fifteen. Next, meet girl group the Shirelles, who brought their close **harmonies** and R&B sound to larger audiences than female musicans had ever had before. Next, the Runaways: this all-girl five-piece got together when they were teenagers and exploded the expectations about what a girl could do on stage, making inroads into heavy metal and punk. Finally, ESG, a group of sisters from the Bronx whose original style and sound still influences bands today.

JANis MARTIn

Janis Martin was born in Virginia in 1940, and started playing the guitar when she was four years old. Like with many young girls, her family played an important role in

encouraging Janis to play the guitar and to sing in front of people. Her dad and uncle were both musicians, and her mother was very supportive of her career. Her family entered her into all the contests she could play, and by the time she was eleven years old, she was playing on a weekly radio show called the *WDVA Barn Dance,* a country music variety show. By the time she was thirteen, she was performing with well-known country music singers like Jean Shepard and Ernest Tubb, and had discovered R&B music.

Janis Martin combined her guitar skills, sassy singing voice, and charismatic stage presence to explore a new kind of music, which was being called "rockabilly" because it combined rock and country, or "hillbilly," music. At fifteen, she signed with RCA Records—just two months after they signed a guy named Elvis Presley. The record label knew that the rockabilly sound was gaining in popularity, and they saw that Janis had the skills to make her way—but they saw even more profit in the idea of marketing her as "the female Elvis," a label she was never happy with.

When she was sixteen, Janis released her debut record with RCA, called "Willyou, Willyum." The B-side of that record, which she wrote herself, was called "Drugstore Rock 'n' Roll," and that song sold 750,000 copies and was a hit on both the pop and country charts. Janis also appeared at the Grand Ole Opry (as one of the youngest performers ever) as well as on *American Bandstand.* She also won *Billboard* magazine's "Most Promising Female Vocalist" award in 1956.

Even though she was reaching the height of her career, Janis didn't have very much control over her life. Her career was directed by her manager and her family, and she never had much of a chance to be a normal teenager. This was undoubtedly frustrating for someone with such a big personality and energetic style. She had a boyfriend, though, with whom she secretly eloped when she was only fifteen. She got pregnant not long after that, and as a result of her pregnancy her record label dropped her. (In the 1970s, Janis returned to performing and gained a massive following in Europe, where she played rockabilly revival shows. She continued to perform and record until her death in 2007.)

Janis Martin's story is an interesting example of a girl who generated a whole new image for females on stage: She had a strong voice, she played guitar, and she moved around in a way we generally associate with Elvis Presley. But the morality of her time made it impossible for her to grow up and still have success as a musician; motherhood then was almost inescapably the same as retiring from stage life. But she remains an inspiration, because as a very young person, she was able to play the kind of music she liked and really rock the house.

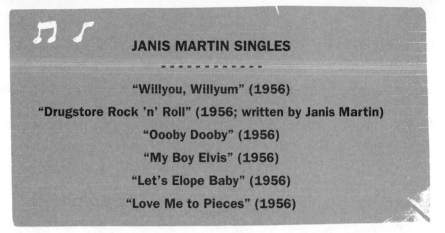

JANIS MARTIN SINGLES

- - - - - - - - - - - -

"Willyou, Willyum" (1956)

"Drugstore Rock 'n' Roll" (1956; written by Janis Martin)

"Oooby Dooby" (1956)

"My Boy Elvis" (1956)

"Let's Elope Baby" (1956)

"Love Me to Pieces" (1956)

▶▶ When you think about young girls who are making an impact in the music industry now, what problems do you see that they encounter when they grow up to be young women? Are these problems similar or different from what you have experienced?

▶▶ Do you think Janis Martin rebelled against stereotypes of being a girl?

THE SHiRELLeS

When you think of "girl groups," what do you think of? Girl groups were a phenomenon that changed forever the way girls and women participate in the music industry in the United States. Groups such as the Shirelles, the Ronettes, and the Shangri-Las were made up of young women, often in their teens, who recorded and performed with great success all over the country. And for every girl group you have heard of, there are probably ten you haven't. Singing together and playing music was a hobby for many girls who never cut records or performed on the stage.

In the early 1960s, as rock 'n' roll was gaining momentum in the United States, girls from all over the country wanted to participate. Like Janis Martin, many of them had learned about music from a very young age, from their families, from church, and from listening to the radio. The Shirelles was a singing group made up of four friends: Shirley Alston Reeves (who was the main lead singer), Doris Jackson, Beverly Lee, and Addie "Micki" Harris. The girls met at their school in New Jersey in 1958 and at first called themselves the Poquellos. They wrote a song called "I Met Him on a Sunday" and entered their school talent show with it. They made such an impression on their friends that one asked them to audition for her mother, Florence Greenberg, who had a small record label. Florence became their manager, coined them a new name (made by combining Shirley's first name with a popular doo-wop group from the time called the Chantels), and got "I Met Him on a Sunday" signed to Decca, an important record label.

The Shirelles' career had its ups and downs, alternating hits and flops. They recorded music they wrote, and also sang music written by popular songwriters of the time, such as Gerry Goffin and Carole King, Burt Bacharach and Hal David, and Van McCoy. Their real commercial success came in 1961, when the song "Will You Love Me Tomorrow?" made it to the number-one position on the pop charts, and to number two on the R&B charts. The Shirelles were the first all-girl group to accomplish this feat.

The Shirelles were also important because their musical style combined doo-wop singing styles with R&B, and therefore their music appealed to both white and African American audiences. They sang songs that addressed things that girls were interested in and concerned about. "Will You Love Me Tomorrow" explains the anxiety of a girl who is caught between her own desires and the restrictive morality of her time. She's afraid that if she makes out with a boy, or even has sex with him, he will like it but then judge her negatively about it later. As girls and women began to gain more control over their own bodies and lives in the 1960s, they could not always count on the rest of the world to be on the same page with them. The Shirelles talked about these problems in ways girls could relate to, and that everyone could dance to.

♫ ♪ **THE SHIRELLES SINGLES**

- - - - - - - - - - - -

"I Met Him on a Sunday" (1958; written by the Shirelles)
"Will You Love Me Tomorrow?" (1960)
"Mama Said" (1961)
"Soldier Boy" (1962)
"Baby It's You" (1962)
"Foolish Little Girl" (1963)
"Sha-La-La" (1964)

▶ Do you play music with your friends from school? Who at your school do you think you could play music with?

▶ What artists do you listen to who sing about subjects that confuse or worry you, or make you feel anxious? How does listening to this music make you feel better or more relaxed?

THe RUNaways

The Runaways also got together as teenagers and started out in Southern California in 1975 with Kari Krome, Joan Jett, Micki Steele, and Sandy West. Soon Lita Ford, Cherie Currie, and Jacki Fox joined the band, and Micki left. The Runaways had a tough-girl look, with tight leather clothes and long hair. On stage they emulated emerging heavy metal and punk bands, singing loudly and playing their music energetically.

The Runaways formed at a very different time than the Shirelles; even though it was only fifteen years later, a lot had changed for girls and women in America. The Runaways had a very tough, sexually self-confident way of presenting themselves on stage. Unlike the challenges in the '50s and '60s of fitting into expectations for the behavior of girls and women, even when they were stars on stage, the Runaways didn't care if people thought they were mean or aggressive—that's what they wanted people to think!

The Runaways did have one strong outside force to deal with: their manager, whose name was Kim Fowley. He worked with the girls to create the band that eventually went on to have success, but it's a common misconception that he brought them together as a "tough girl" novelty act. The talent and the initial ideas for the band came from the girls themselves.

In 1976, the Runaways signed to Mercury Records and released their first album, *The Runaways.* They toured the United States, playing numerous sold-out shows and securing their place with other rock bands both in England and all over the United States. In 1977, the Runaways toured in Japan, and their record went to number three, behind Led Zeppelin and Kiss.

By 1978 the lineup of the band had changed a lot, and the members fought with their manager about money and how the band was being run. By 1979, the band had broken up. Members of the band (especially Joan Jett and Lita Ford) went on to successful solo careers.[2]

The Runaways played a style of music that mixed heavy metal, rock, and punk. They were very loud and confrontational, and many of their lyrics are anti-establishment (anti-family, -school, -work, etc.). This approach created a wildly successful live act, but it did not translate into record sales. Additionally, the image the band put forward of tough-girls-on-the-run was easy for the rock press to ignore or scorn.

The Runaways were important in the history of girls in rock because of their outspoken toughness and their image as girls who took their power and used it

---

2 - The Sandy West Foundation was created after the passing of Sandy West. Part of its mission is to contribute money to the Rock 'n' Roll Camp for Girls in Portland to support drummers.

how they wanted: to make loud and aggressive music, and to sing about what they thought was wrong with the world.

THE RUNAWAYS RECORDS

- - - - - - - - - - - -

The Runaways (1976) LP
Queens of Noise (1977) LP
Waitin' for the Night (1977) LP
Little Lost Girls (1981) LP

➡ Can you think of girls playing music now who have a "tough" image? What does that mean, and do you think it is important? Why?

➡ Which bands do you know who sing about what is wrong with the world? How do they express it? Do you think they get it right?

esg

Around the same time that the Runaways were calling it quits, a resourceful and creative mother in the South Bronx bought her four daughters musical instruments. She did this in part because she and her husband were both musical people, but she also saw music as a way to focus the talents and energies of her children, Renee, Deborah, Valerie, and Marie Scroggins. The streets of the South Bronx, she reasoned, were not as safe as staying inside, jamming.

When they first started out, Renee, the eldest, was eleven years old. The girls had already started using pots and pans to make music, so it was not long before they started playing the drums and singing together. The four sisters played in a variety of lineups that included their cousins, Larry and Tito, as well as Leroy Glover and David Miles. They came up with their name from a combination of their birthstones—emerald and sapphire, plus gold.

When the sisters were young, they watched TV and learned cover songs by bands like the Rolling Stones. But they soon started writing their own music, which had an entirely new sound. It had rock influences, but it also had a heavy Latin rhythmic sound, with sparse guitar and funky bass. ESG was one of the first bands to play house music, hip-hop, and punk in an exciting new combination. ESG started their career by playing talent shows. Their new sound was recognized and appreciated by people in the dance scene in New York City. Soon they released their first single,

"Moody," produced by Englishman Martin Hannett, who was famous for his work with the band Joy Division.

ESG's music is based around complex polyrhythms and simple, yet catchy, melodies. Because of this, they are one of the most frequently sampled bands in hip-hop. Some of the more than fifty bands who have used small sections of beats or melodies from their songs include TLC, the Beastie Boys, Big Daddy Kane, and the Wu-Tang Clan. Although this has made their music very familiar and recognizable, it wasn't until the 1990s that ESG started getting both credit and money for their original work. (They even put out a record in 1993 called *Sample Credits Don't Pay Our Bills*.)

ESG never had any big hits, but their career intersected with the worlds of punk and hip-hop in some very unique ways. As teenagers, they played shows with the Clash, Grandmaster Flash, and Gang of Four. They also played in some famous dance and rock clubs, including the Paradise Garage in New York City and the Hacienda in Manchester, England. Their consistent strength was staying true to their own sound, never changing to please anyone else, including managers, producers, or record labels.

ESG was a band for over thirty years, and in one incarnation even included the daughters of two of the original members, who started playing with their moms when they were teenagers. ESG played their last show in September 2007, but their unique sound will remain influential. Check them out!

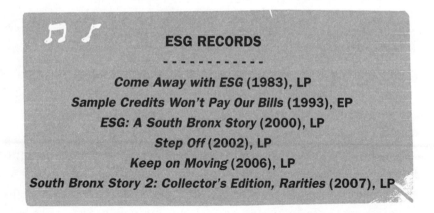

ESG RECORDS

- - - - - - - - - - - -

Come Away with ESG (1983), LP
Sample Credits Won't Pay Our Bills (1993), EP
ESG: A South Bronx Story (2000), LP
Step Off (2002), LP
Keep on Moving (2006), LP
South Bronx Story 2: Collector's Edition, Rarities (2007), LP

➤➤ Do you have similar musical tastes to people in your family? How and why are your tastes the same or different?

➤➤ Can you think of any songs that use samples by girl musicians? What about girl musicians who use other people's samples as part of their music?

WHy I'M NOT a Rock St★r

BY CYNTHIA NELSON

I never like it when people call me a rock star, or assume that I want to be one just because I am a musician. It always has this kind of connotation that seems negative to me. I never began playing music because I wanted to be a rock star. It was just something that I was drawn to do and loved doing from the beginning. There is so much more to playing music than becoming a rock star. I do it for the recognition within myself that happens when I sing or play music, I learn more about my own soul and who I am. It is not in desire to be acknowledged from the outside that I play music. It always makes me cringe whenever anyone is talking about wanting to become famous, because I think this has nothing to do with the art of music, but more to do with ego gratification.

—Brooke Gillespie, The Holy Experiment/Isle of Citadel

I cannot count the number of times I have been introduced to someone new by a well-meaning friend, "This is Cynthia. She's a rock star." What they are trying to do is explain something about what I do with my time, wrapped in what they perceive as a compliment about my abilities or level of success in my endeavors. Despite people's good intentions, when I am referred to as a rock star I feel frustrated, misunderstood, and, given my level of actual "rock stardom" or success in music with regard to fame, actually more like a failure. I am not a rock star, nor do I seek to be one. I am a rock musician, a songwriter, a multi-instrumentalist, and now a music teacher. If you want to give me a compliment, call me an artist.

What is a rock star? Is it someone whose music has made them famous, someone who carries herself with a certain amount of charisma, fashion sense, and self-selling bravado, or someone whose music is popular regardless of their personality? The term "rock star" in today's pop culture lexicon can refer to anything from an outstanding person in any field to a certain caffeinated energy beverage. But when the name is applied to someone who takes rock music seriously as their calling, the term might demean their calling, overlook their intentions, and drown their passions.

Who doesn't want to be a rock star? Attention, glory, money, travel, and, most irresistibly, worldwide distribution and appreciation of one's songs (creative efforts contextualized and rewarded!) seem nice. But if these are my goals, I will always be falling short. Calling myself a rock musician means I am right on track, always doing it well, and striving to make better and more interesting music for its own sake. I can share the music or not as I see fit, play with others or alone. I am living in the moment and I am happy.

I reject the notion that fame and glory are an integral part of rock or "popular" music. I am not a rock star because I aim to make music that may be insular, complex, beautiful, weird, and not for everyone. I am not a rock star because I play music for music's sake and for my sake and for my friends. And for you, if you want to hear it, and if not, I am still playing.

...testimonial...

Being in a girl band creates a code of solidarity that inspires girls to do things for one another and as a group in a generative and challenging way. In watching bandmates interact, I have noticed that girls do not focus on weaknesses, like someone playing the wrong guitar note constantly, but tend to shift their attention to what is "cool" about the song, or how to make a riff more accessible to everyone. Girls are not daunted by failure when they are in an environment that supports whatever action they take; girls are willing to take risks, willing to make mistakes, and willing to look silly when they are rewarded for putting themselves out there.

The center principles of rock music remind me to always try to make better music, to be less critical of myself and others, and to play music simply because it feels good. I continue coming back to the Portland Rock 'n' Roll Camp for Girls to work because it is such a fundamentally important space in our society, and a truly revolutionary event in history.

Emma McKenna

How do you get started playing an instrument or writing a song? Where do you find your voice and the inspiration to use it?

How do you know if you're doing it right?

There's more to making music than just playing the right notes at the right time. Every person, and every instrument, has their own special and unique voice. Being a musician means immersing yourself in the process of unlocking those voices, of listening deeply to sounds, patterns, pitches, and tones and developing techniques to generate and communicate your own style, voice, and aesthetic.

Playing music is a journey of discovery and exploration that can last your whole life. In this chapter we cover aspects of what makes each instrument unique, how to approach playing with other people, and how to get started in the songwriting process.

TO ALL You GENIUS Future Songwriters

BY KAIA WILSON

HEY! Pay attention! I know some of you will start totally spacing out in about ten minutes but I SWEAR you will LOVE writing songs and I am going to lay it down right here.

Bottom line: It's EASY to write a song, HARD to write a good song. But I have enormous amounts of confidence that you (that's right, *you*) can do it.

Here are some tips for getting started:

DO experiment. Let go of judging yourself, have fun, get excited, believe that you have written the best song ever.

DO NOT expect immediate brilliance. **DO NOT** be discouraged by the fact that you, along with the rest of us (and this does include the WHITE STRIPES) will write some not-so-great songs.

DO keep trying. Write songs for yourself, perform huge concerts for yourself in your bedroom . . . let yourself be free to do/think/say whatever it is you want to when you write a song.

DO NOT leave your journal full of lyrics at a coffee shop.

When you break it down, there are really just four steps to songwriting.

(1.) Inspiration
(2.) Melody
(3.) Lyrics
(4.) Song Structure

(It's that simple.)

Inspiration

To write a song, you need a subject (from world problems to the kitchen sink) or motivated feeling (joy, anger, confusion, an activity you're passionate about—heartbreak works wonders) and then a melody, some lyrics, and POOF! Here's an example:

Cindy's pet hamster, Mr. Little Face, died of old age one day and Cindy felt very sad. So she picked up her Gibson Les Paul guitar and slammed down a wicked rad melody, complete with a forty-two-measure SMOKIN' guitar-solo-fret-attack with the following lyrics:

Oh Mr. Little Face,
It was you and only you,
Who would run around in a wheel for hours
And never seem to stop and smell the flowers.

Oh Mr. Little Face,
I will love you forever,
I know someday we will be together.
Mr. Little Face, Mr. Little Face
I love you it's so true.

Melody

Melodies can come out of anywhere—they might just fly into your mind and you open your mouth and start to sing, or you might be fiddling around with your musical instrument and find something that you think rules and go from there. All you really need to write a good melody is to GO FOR IT—keep singing and playing until something sounds right.

Lyrics

Lyrics are a hugely important part of a song, but there aren't any rules. Lyrics can be about anything, or they can make no sense at all. They can rhyme, or they can almost rhyme, or they can *not* rhyme at all! Again, just start writing until something sounds right to you. It's like anything you learn and create—you just have to practice and practice and you have to START somewhere and see where it takes you.

While you should know your theme or subject, lyrics can be as obvious or as cryptic as you want. They can be written in a direct, rhyming way:

> I was walking all funnylike to the store
> when I jumped into a soccer game to make the winning score
> then I went home fell asleep and began to snore

or in a more ABSTRACT, not-so-rhyming way:

> In the sun, panthers, I could not tell you at the time,
> falling is this the dimension? Is this home?
> Candles . . . barn . . . hackysack . . .
> DON'T PUT MY SWEATER IN THE DRYER!

Rhyming is not essential in songwriting, but it can be nice; there's something about rhyme that seems to complete a rhythm. But remember, when you're looking for the right word, you can write lyrics that ALMOST rhyme and sound good:

> When will I see the moon,
> and when will I see you,
> dancing among the stars
> keeps me from falling apart

You can write lyrics in your journal, on the computer, on a napkin. You can write lyrics before a melody is written, or after you already have instrument melodies or a melody in your head. When I am writing a song, lyrics come last in my process. I write a guitar melody first, then sing nonsense words like "meow meow meow" or "la la la" or "blah dad a duuu poo doo braaaap," and then finally fit lyrics into the vocal melody I create.

You can write about anything in the world that you want to. You can write intuitively, writing whatever pops out of your head without "thinking," or you can think and think and think about what you want to say.

So, those are the first three steps to a good little kernel of a song. But actually, there is one more part that takes it to the next level. . .

Song Structure

Song structure, or arrangement, is the name for what order the parts of the song are in and how many times they are repeated, among other things.

There are patterns or structures or formulas for all songs, and they can be very different from song to song. You can make up whatever structure you want for your song, or you can follow the most common approach; it's up to you.

Many songs are written in the following structure:

1. VERSE 1

Generally the first verse is a melody hook. The music is usually played in a way that creates a sense of building or rising, so that when you get to the chorus you can make it the BIG part of the song.

2. CHORUS

The chorus is the hookiest part of the song, something catchy that you want to sing along to, of course, because it's the part that repeats. This is where the music tends to get louder and more full sounding, where the vocal melody can get more dynamic (more high notes, swooping down to low notes then back up to high notes, for example) and the lyrics express the MAIN point of what the song is about.

3. VERSE 2

Getting back into the lyrical storytelling (or not, because maybe you want to write very abstract, strange lyrics), this verse is often shorter than the first verse in length and maybe adds another instrument variation (like a xylophone or a nose flute or a tuba).

That brings me to a note on instrumentation: This is the name for deciding which instruments are used in a particular song, and when and how they appear. Which instruments you choose—guitar with fuzz box or piano or autoharp—can have as big

an impact on how the song feels as how it sounds. It can be fun and inspiring to think about instrumentation while you're writing. Think, what would sound good on this melody? What instrument sort of matches my theme?

4. CHORUS

Often, the second time the chorus comes into the song, it repeats its length (double it up!), just to tell the audience "I AM THE CHORUS: Sing along!"

5. BRIDGE OR BREAKDOWN

The bridge in a song is where, after the second chorus, there's an entirely new melody introduced. It usually only happens once, and may be very different in mood, key, or dynamic. A great bridge is a thrilling moment in a song. The bridge is often also the place where you will hear a "solo" of the guitar/sax/nose flute sort, often followed by a vocal melody that gets all big and finds a good way to transition nicely into the final chorus.

The breakdown is just like it sounds: instruments drop out, or the music gets all quiet, or stripped down, or just different sounding. For a breakdown, usually the melody repeats the verse melody, so that the listener recognizes it in its new, stripped-down form, like just bass and drums, and then the whole thing builds back up and crescendos into the final chorus.

6. FINAL, SPINE-TINGLING, JUMPING-UP-AND-DOWN CHORUS

The last chorus is HUGE. I mean, this is where you lay down all the magic you can offer. The last chorus repeats at least two times, but often three or four times, and it can go on fifty million times until you fade it out. . . . If it's a solo song, you do something slightly different with your voice and instrument, playing so that the chorus sounds bigger or more INTENSE. If you're in a band, you throw in the cowbell, tambourine, extra-crazy guitar and/or keyboard parts, drum madness, watermelon rind—ANYTHING that will make that last chorus go out with a bang. Like, "SINCE YOU'VE BEEN GO-OO-OO-OO-NE!!!!!!" You know how it is.

You can make up different song structures for your own songs; you can even write a song that is one long verse, or one long chorus . . . if you are Bob Dylan, you would write a song with twelve verses and twelve choruses. Any way you want to write is AWESOME—you can make up an entirely new way of writing a song or go with the tried and true.

ROCK 'N' ROLE MODELS

Here's a good exercise for getting started writing a song. Think of one of your favorite songs. Then, try to write a song melody and structure that is similar but different enough from that song so that it's still your own. To do this you will need to learn how to play your favorite song, or at least really understand the structure of the song, and then you can create a melody in that same vein.

Write your own lyrics, in your own way, without copying your favorite song's lyrical style. This is your homework, but it will not be graded and you never have to turn it in. How rad is that? Just go home, listen to your fave song over and over, figure out the melody and structure, write your own melody and structure that is similar but still your own, then write some lyrics. . . .

Now, learn how to play all your favorite songs! The more you practice playing and writing, the sooner you will begin creating your own writing style. It is really superfun and thrilling to be able to say, "I wrote this song!"

tHE WRiTiNG iS FRee

by Cynthia Nelson

Have you ever written a song?

How did you do it? (There are a million ways to do it.)

Do you hear music first or words first?

What kinds of things are songs about?

What kinds of things are YOUR songs about?

Can you imagine a kind of song that you've never heard before or that no one's ever written before? What does it sound like? What is the instrumentation? How is it **arranged?**

Take some time to analyze the lyrics to a few of your favorite songs. What do you like about them? Is there a word or a line you wish were different, less predictable?

My favorite thing in lyrics is when I am surprised by the rhyme. If I can predict the words before they happen, most likely the songwriter relied on a rhyming cliché. What are some rhyming clichés?

Cynthia's Personal List of Rhyming Clichés:

➡ *home, all alone,* and *phone*

➡ *Don't go away* and *Please stay*

➡ *I love you* and *My heart is true*

Make your own list:

_____

_____

_____

_____

_____

_____

There are also subject matter clichés, like writing about love relationships or partying. Personally, I think it's easier to do something new with tired subject matter than to revive a rhyming cliché.

To get started writing, sometimes I like to read poetry that is inspiring and then do a freewrite: I write nonstop, without judging or questioning. Sometimes I am thinking about a theme when I freewrite, but often I just let my pen do the talking. Then I go back and find the central theme of my own blah-blahing and hone in on that as my subject. Sometimes I think of a subject I want to write a song about, or a title, long before I write lyrics.

Whether you start with an idea or a completely blank slate, remember to think of words as tools for being yourself and expressing your ideas and feelings. This can also mean being completely abstract or writing about or from the perspective of another character, real or imagined, but in your own way. Try to choose words and word combinations that no one else has thought of putting to paper or in a song. Keep working on it and try again!

. . . testimonial . . .

I used to think making music was impossibly magical, a boat I missed in my youth, but working at Rock Camp and seeing girl after girl sit at her drum set like a queen on her throne slowly made me think, "Hey, maybe I can do this." I asked a particularly skilled camper how long it took her to get that good. She said about two years. Okay then, I thought, that's my goal. Just like that.

One particular girl changed my life. She pounded her drums so hard they would creep away from her constantly while her cymbals simultaneously unhinged. When she finally noticed, she giggled with delight, not at all apologetic, fixed the gear, and did it all again. She focused hard on her counts, sweated up a storm, and messed up over and over again, but was never deterred. Watching her, I came to realize that messing up is part of the fun!

What if I lived my life like these girls live in Rock Camp? Can I re-create a nine-year-old's fearlessness in my life—with music and everything else?

Claudia Lucero

HOW TO Sound LIKE a VACUUM CLEANER

BY BETH DITTO

I learned about pitch from the monotone hum of the vacuum cleaner during Sunday cleaning. In daycare, while the other kids loathed naptime, I looked forward to it. While I lay on my cot, the ladies with their big hair and long, painted nails turned the knob on the radio to the local country station. I lay under the safe watch of Mrs. Mary, Mrs. Shirley, and another young lady who loved Randy Travis. We all waited for our favorite song. Even though I had a Pink Floyd–loving mom who hated country music, especially Randy Travis, I waited every day for my song. "I'm Digging Up Bones," a solid-gold country number-one hit of the time, would come on in less than a minute every time. I couldn't care less about Randy Travis, but those eight beats at the beginning of the song were like a feast: first the thick fat bass line, then the heavy thump-thump-thump caught my ear, and then the guitar line, sweet and simple, just like my tiny hometown of Judsonia itself. Then the singing started and my little four-measure song ended. I still write songs this way, proving that this time of my life was crucial. I picked up everything I needed to know about music by the age of four.

When I was eight, my brother got drums for Christmas. I was heartbroken. It's important to me to point out that it isn't our ability that denies us the chance to make music, it's something much older and much harder to understand when you're eight and tapping out beats on the back of a chair while your brother's in the other room doing the real thing.

I longed to be a musician, but although I was only a little girl, I knew that I shouldn't dare dream of being a singer because I thought I wasn't pretty enough—as if that were true and as if that mattered! (Fifteen years later, I am on a plane from London discussing with my friend whether or not I should do a Gap ad.)

When I was little I got called "slow" a lot. I wasn't especially good in school. My brain liked to run off all the time. It couldn't stand the droning of the teacher's voices. The black numbers on the white paper bored me to tears, so my mind would flee to music. There was always a ditty. During the most boring parts of school or in the scariest parts of nighttime there was always a tune to entertain and soothe.

It's a long way from those confusing days to my current career as a singer. But I never cared what people thought of me much—until I began vocal instruction at Rock Camp. I usually spend about a week preparing to teach a workshop for the girls. I make these little lessons and have elaborate plans in mind, but just as soon as the class starts their mouths open and all the ideas I have about structure are gone.

There are many different voices—both typical and trained, soft and loud, harsh and mellow. I forget in the midst of all their best efforts and shyness that I have any agenda at all. I play them Yoko Ono, with her shrill vibrato, and I tell them, *This is singing, too.* I play Nina Hagen, with her throaty *Exorcist*-esque voice, and say, *This is beautiful.* At a certain point I question why Bob Dylan is considered genius and Yoko considered crazy. I play Antony and the Johnsons and Nina Simone back to back and ask, which is the boy and which is the girl? Most of the time, they cannot tell, and all I have to say is, *See? It doesn't matter which is which.* The song is still a song, and it is beautiful.

It's important to listen with an all-new pair of ears and see with an all-new set of eyes. Then the ideas of what is an acceptable voice are broken down to allow for

variety—something missing from most girls raised on popular music. I love instructing girls at such a formative age because you have a lot of power, but by far, the most empowering part of it all is taking none away from them.

Girls, playing any instrument is hard. But when it is attached by muscle and tissue to your body, like your voice is, there is no comparison to just how personal it is. Your instrument is your body. And being a part of this world, we all know that hardly anything is subject to more criticism than the female body. The whole thing: the feet, the hands, the face, and the mind. When you sing, you claim your body back. Everything goes out of your throat, over your tongue, and through your teeth out into the world. Once it's out there, you can't take it back. It's caught in the ears of others.

OBSESSED WITH SOUND
by Kate Walsh

Ever since I was a kid I've been tuned in to the idea of sound—sound as music, sounds in our modern world, little sounds, big sounds, new sounds, nostalgic sounds. When I was seven, I named my cat 'Puter because she sounded like our Apple II GS disk drive when she purred. I used to sing with the vacuum cleaner, dishwasher, dryer, heater, computer, TV buzz, and other household appliances, trying to match the pitch with my voice. When I got older, I even started to **harmonize** with them.

Fast-forward to my high school days, when I was in jazz band, concert band, and **music theory** class. I was obsessed, my focus wandering from the actual quality and timbre of a sound to the way it was presented in relation to other sounds within a piece of music. I delved into the nitty-gritty of harmony and jazz theory, trying to decipher notes and chords and progressions to uncover the big secret that makes music the most powerful thing in my world. I wanted to know what made some progressions catchy and others not, how songs could be happy and sad at the same time, and, most important, how I could write more amazing songs myself.

But, as the cliché goes, the more I learned about music theory, the less I understood about the power of music. The questions remained, even if they got more specific. Why was a **I-IV-V** progression more powerful in one song than another? Why did the songs I wrote sound better on an organ than on an upright piano?

Searching for answers to these impossible questions exposed me to lots of different music, and made me realize one thing: I love all of it. I love pop. I love soul. I love punk rock. I love reggae, rock-steady, and gospel. All these types of music use exactly the same **chords**, instruments, and melodies and they all have the same foundation: sound.

The impact of a song often depends on the quality of sound produced by the various instruments and voices involved. Sound quality is about the difference between a Rhodes electric piano and a Wurlitzer organ, an old **tube amp** and a new **solid-state** amp, an echo box that works by warping magnetic tape and a modern pedal that uses computer chips. It's about **falsetto** or **head voice**, or **acoustic** vs. electric guitar. A band I'm in now uses no **digital** equipment. We use no digital effects, and record only on tape; everything is **analog**. I've come to appreciate the aesthetic, even if I have to drag the Rhodes up two or three flights of stairs.

Instead of starting to write songs with the chords and **scales** you learned from your instrument teacher, try finding a sound on your instrument that you really like. What do you like about it? Why? Try an effects pedal. What do you like or dislike about those sounds? It doesn't matter what notes you play; just think about the sound. Once you find a sound you really enjoy and want to play over and over again, start thinking about different notes and melodies. How many different sounds can you get out of a snare drum? Play every ride cymbal at the music store and ask yourself which one you like best. Which guitar, bass, keyboard, or microphone sounds best to you? Even if you don't know much about equipment, you know what sounds you like, and what sounds you don't. You know what sounds you want to hear when you're feeling a particular way.

The point is, don't compromise on sound. Adjust your amp, guitar, keyboard, drum set, bass, **PA**, microphone, **MIDI** sound—whatever it is—until you are completely satisfied with it. The possibilities are literally infinite.

PICK UP A GUITAR and PLAY

BY MARISA ANDERSON

Choosing a Guitar

So you play the guitar, or you want to play the guitar. Maybe you inherited an acoustic guitar that's been sitting in your uncle/dad/grandma's closet for twenty years. Maybe you went to the music store and ogled, the most amazing red-flamed, shiny guitar with knobs and dials all over it. Or maybe you stared at the wall of guitars for an hour wondering how on earth to pick the right one when there are so many different kinds.

HOW DO I KNOW IF A GUITAR IS RIGHT FOR ME?

Before you choose a guitar, think about the music that you like. What kind of guitar is being played with that music? Watch and listen to music, notice the guitars used to make it. Just like different singers have different voices, different guitars make different sounds. A Fender Stratocaster will sound clean and clear, a Telecaster will be more twangy. A Gibson Les Paul or an SG will be crunchier and more distorted. Or maybe you want to play an acoustic guitar and get the more organic sound of strings and wood with no electronics.

THE TEST DRIVE

Your guitar should be easy to hold—comfortable on your lap while you're sitting, and not too heavy when you are standing. You should like how it looks: the color and shape. You should be able to comfortably reach the tuning pegs, and when you rest your thumb against the back of the neck, your fingers should be able to reach every string.

When you go to buy a guitar, take your time in the store. Play a bunch of different guitars. Don't hurry. Even if you don't know how to play, sit with a few different guitars. Put the strap over your shoulders and stand up. Run your hands up and down it to get a feel for the guitar you are holding. If you can, bring someone who knows how to play a little and listen to the sounds of the different guitars; just like people, each guitar has its own voice, and they can vary dramatically. Plug in and play the guitar through an amp. Lots of stores have private rooms where you can try out guitars.

Don't be afraid to ask questions. Music stores can be intimidating even for experienced musicians. The presence of a supportive friend, even one who does not know very much about buying instruments, can be reassuring. Buying a guitar is a personal thing—there are as many opinions on what a good guitar sounds like as there are players.

IMPORTANT MECHANICS

Once you've narrowed the field to a few guitars you like for their sound and style, it's time to look critically at a couple of important factors. First of all, check the distance between the strings and the fret board—this is called the **action**. If the action is really high—that is, if the strings are more than about a quarter of an inch above the fret board—the guitar is going to be hard to play. Conversely, if the action is too low—if the strings look like they are touching the frets—the guitar will buzz and rattle and not sound good. If you find a guitar you love and the action doesn't feel right to you, do not worry—adjusting the action is usually a quick and easy job for a repairperson to do, and is often included when you're buying a guitar. But be cautious; if the action can't be adjusted to a comfortable playing level, you might be looking at a deeper problem, such as a bad neck, and you should probably walk away from that instrument.

The second important factor to evaluate is if the neck of the guitar is straight and level. If the guitar neck is warped, the guitar will not be tunable. It can be hard to tell, but if you hold the guitar at eye level with the body facing toward you and the neck stretched out away from you, so that as you are looking down the length of the neck it looks like a road running away from you, the fret wires (those metal bands along the guitar neck) should all appear perfectly parallel. If the fret wires look uneven or tilt away from each other, move on to the next guitar.

Starting to Play

TUNING

Start by getting in tune. In the beginning, a tuner is your best friend. Plug into the input and tune the strings EADGBE, moving from the fattest to the skinniest string.

CHORD CHARTS AND TABLATURE

Lots of people teach themselves to play guitar. Two of the best resources you can have to start learning guitar are a chord chart and an understanding of tablature.

Chords are groups of three or more notes and they are written as letters and numbers, such as Am or D7. It's not so important when you are starting out to know exactly what the letters and numbers mean; you just need to be able to play them. To help with this, the chord names are sometimes accompanied by a small diagram with lines and dots to show you what the chord looks like on the fret board.

In the following chord chart, the horizontal lines represent frets, the vertical lines represent strings, and the dots are where you put your fingers.

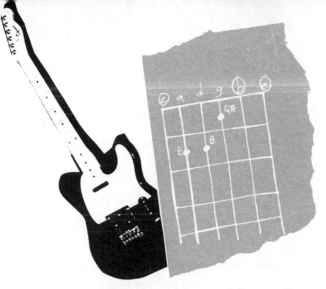

Note how the picture shows the guitar as if you were holding it upright and facing you. There is a chord chart "on pages 182 and 183" with lots of commonly used chords.

Guitar music is often written in a system called "tab" (short for tablature). This system is very accessible and is used by a lot of people, especially when posting songs on the Internet. Tab is a picture of the strings with numbers on them referring to the frets where you put your fingers. For example, the number 3 on the line labeled E means that you put your finger on the third fret of the E string. When it reads 0, that means play it open—don't press any fret when you play that string. When you see numbers written in a stack, press all those frets at the same time. Read across the page from left to right.

While you are learning to play, it is important to develop the muscles in all four fingers of your left hand. Generally you can move around the fret board finger by finger, so that if your middle finger is planted on the third fret, you can use your index finger for any note on the second fret, and your ring finger for any note on the fourth or fifth fret. Challenge your pinky to stay in the game—the more fingers you have control of, the more fluid your guitar playing will be.

Here is an example of tab:

```
E----------------------------------------------------0---2---3-
B--------------------------------------0----1----3------------3-
G-----------------------------0--2--------------------------0-
D-------------------0---2---4---------------------------------
A----------0---2----3-----------------------------------------
E------3------------------------------------------------------
```

It's important to remember that in written music, low sounds are written on the bottom, and high sounds are written on top, regardless of where you might find these sounds on your instrument. This means that guitar tab is written upside down. The low E string is the fat string up by your chest, and the high E string is the skinny one down by your stomach. A good mnemonic device for remembering the string names goes like this: Eat A Darn Good Breakfast Early (starting with a low E and ending with a high E).

You can decide whether to use your fingers or a pick when you play the guitar. Again, it's a matter of personal preference. It's good to be versatile, so being able to play either way is best, because different styles call for different techniques. For example, fast punk strumming is easiest to accomplish with a pick in your right hand, while a song where you play the strings one at a time in a pattern might sound better when you play with your fingers.

STRUMMING

Strumming the guitar is a common way to accompany yourself or another person while they are singing a song. Strumming is accomplished by brushing your right hand or a pick across the strings while making a chord with your left hand. Strumming is usually done in a pattern of up strokes (your hand moves up across the strings) and down strokes (your hand moves down over the strings).

For a guitar player, the rhythm of a song is often carried by strumming in a pattern. In the beginning, an easy guitar strum looks like this: ↓↓↓↓. Strum down while counting "one, two, three, four" out loud. Tap your foot in time. When learning more advanced strumming patterns, a good tool for steadiness and memorization of the pattern is to say it out loud in the rhythm of the strum, like this: "down down up down down up." This can also be written ↓↓↑↓↓↑.

Tap your foot steadily and play this pattern while counting along, repeating over and over "one, two, three, four." Match the down strokes with each foot tap and number. The **upstroke** goes right in between when you say "two" and "three," and again in between "four" and "one." It might take some time, but if you practice, you'll get it and you'll be able to make up your own strums. Eventually you will be able to do this without even thinking about it, and you will be able to turn your attention to switching chords with your left hand.

PLAYING GUITAR AND SINGING AT THE SAME TIME

Practice strumming when you are doing other things, like reading or talking on the phone. See if you can keep a steady strum while you are having a conversation or watching a movie. If you can, then you've succeeded in programming the strum into your kinetic memory, and you're ready to sing and play at the same time.

When you are first trying to sing and play guitar, don't even worry about words, just make sounds or talk; do anything you can to free up your voice from the concentration you are putting into your guitar playing. Get a steady strum going and talk or sing in a way that you think goes with the strum. Work on trying to feel with your voice and your hands the point in your strumming where the pattern starts over. Singing and playing guitar is hard to do at first, but as you practice, it gets easier.

RIFFS, SOLOS, AND SCALES

Another fun way to play guitar is to make up riffs and melodies using one, two, three, or more strings. Some guitarists use scales, others use their ear, and some draw pictures or make patterns on the fret board. Any of these ways of playing is fine, and, just like most things guitar related, being able to combine all of these techniques is the most versatile.

Often when two guitarists are playing together, one of them will be playing the chords to a song and the other one will be soloing or playing notes and riffs. A riff is a short repeated pattern or motif within the music, while a solo is usually a longer, less repetitive musical statement. Riffs often emphasize or complement the rhythm of the song; a solo can be rhythmically freer and might be more evocative of the melody of the song. It's fun to trade back and forth with another guitar player. If you have a friend who plays guitar, you can write a chord progression and take turns playing the chords and making up riffs and solos.

A scale is a succession of tones ascending or descending according to fixed intervals. There are an infinite number of ways to use notes to make up guitar parts, and literally hundreds of scales out there in the world, but there are a few that are used A LOT in rock music. The most commonly used scale when soloing in a rock song is the pentatonic scale. When you play this scale, use all of your fingers, not just your pointer finger.

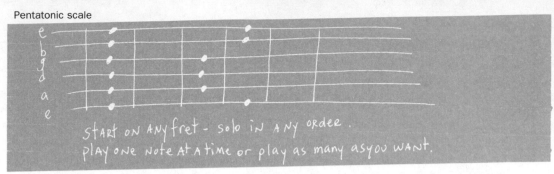

Pentatonic scale

start on any fret - solo in any order. play one note at a time or play as many as you want.

(Remember, the vertical lines are frets and the dots are where you put your fingers. You can start on any fret.)

If scales are easy for you to remember and play—great! Use scale notes, in any order, to build solos and write riffs. You don't have to play the notes one at a time—it sounds cool to mix it up by playing two or three notes at a time. It also sounds cool to purposefully not play scale notes. Dissonance adds texture to music. If scales are boring or confusing for you, DO NOT worry. There are a lot of ways to play guitar.

Patterns and Parts

Almost all music is based on patterns. When you listen to a song or play one with your band, find a pattern of notes that you think goes with the music. Start simply and build. Some people sing notes they think sound good and then find them on their guitar. Pick five notes that sound right to you and play those notes along with the song a few times in a pattern, until it sounds like you've written a little tune inside the song—you've just built a guitar part!

When the song changes parts, say from the verse to the chorus or the verse to the bridge, write another little tune that goes inside the new part. Listen to what the other instruments are doing, especially the vocalist, and build your part so that it doesn't get in the way of what your bandmates are doing. Listen to the drummer and the bass player to get the rhythm of the song.

Some songs have guitar solos, a section where the vocalist lays off and the music has space for the instruments to sing. This is when you can play a pattern or make up new notes that express the energy of the song. Again, remember, speed and volume are fun, but don't forget that music depends on intention and creativity!

Getting Good Sound

Your electric guitar probably has some knobs and switches on it as well as a couple of rectangular boxes underneath the strings. These boxes are called pickups, and they transform the vibrations of the strings into electrical signals that get sent to your

amp and converted into sound. The knobs and switches control which combination of pickups you are using and how loud the sound they are transmitting is. Play around with them and find sounds you like.

If you play electric guitar, an important part of your sound is your amplifier. Learning to use an amp is a process of trial and error. Remember—you are the world's best authority on what sounds good to you! So don't be afraid to try every button and knob on your amp. Turn it up really loud or make it sound crazy and distorted. Have fun experimenting with different string or note combinations, touches, textures, volumes, and effects.

The whole point of playing guitar is to have fun and to build a unique sound. Every skill you learn and every sound you make is one step on the road toward being a versatile musician with a sound and style that is all your own! Go to "Amped: How Do I Get the Sound I Want?" (page 94) for lots more on amplifiers and sound.

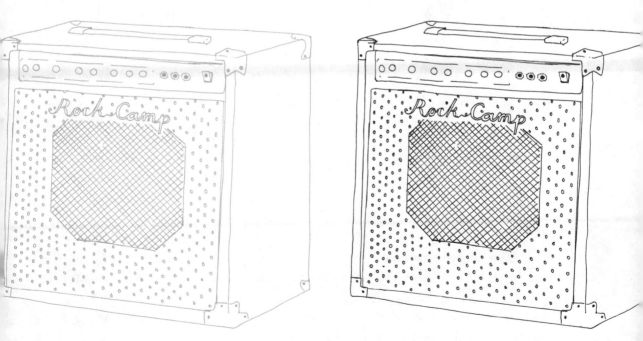

BASS GUiTaR IS GREAT

BY CYNTHIA NELSON

Let me start with some bass basics: There are electric and acoustic bass guitars. There is also the stand-up bass, the orchestra instrument that is sometimes used in rock and can sound pretty cool in a song. But usually you'll see electric bass guitars in rock bands.

Basses are tuned to EADG, from the fattest string to skinniest string. Electric basses require an amp for their sound to be heard. Use a bass amp, not a guitar amp, for the best sound, and so that you don't blow your speaker. It's helpful to have a tuner; most tuners have a bass setting as well as a guitar setting.

The bass is not like a regular guitar, although some people play it that way. The bass is the unifier between the melodic instruments, such as guitar and keyboards, and the rhythmic instruments, such as the drums. The way I see it, in a sense the bass player is the band leader, negotiator, keeper of peace, and creator of harmony. The bass has a lot of potential for emotional expression due to how low the tones go, ringing through the body viscerally. It can be satisfying to make powerful sounds lower than the human voice's potential.

It's important to think about rhythm, which is the way your part goes with or against the drum part. Often the bass strikes notes in time with the kick-drum pattern, so if you're at a loss as to what kind of rhythm to play, try to play at the same time as, or "lock in with," the kick drum. When you are locked in with the drum rhythm, you are playing "in the pocket."

When playing the bass, think about the melody. This is the way in which the notes you choose go with or change the notes or chords of the guitar, keyboards, vocals, and other melodic instruments. Finding the melody and locking in to the rhythm is achieved by LISTENING. Keeping things simple can be as effective or more effective than shredding complexity. Write a simple bass part (a series of notes that sound good to you) and experiment with playing the same thing in a variety of different rhythms.

The **root note** is the first note in the scale, or the name of the chord. Work on locating the root note of the chords or scales your bandmates are playing and start your pattern there. Almost always, if the root sounds good, the fifth will also sound good. The fifth is five steps in the scale above the root. For example, if your root note is C, the fifth is G. If your guitar player or keyboardist is playing a C chord, you can play C and G all day in different rhythms and it will sound great.

The drummer and the bassist working together form the **rhythm section**. Playing in time with the song and everyone else is a big part of the bassist's job. You are the glue. You are holding it together.

If you are writing or learning a song that has more than one part, practice the parts separately, then practice the transition from the end of one part into the beginning of the next part. When the transitions are smooth, play the whole song together. Slow it down to get the smoothness and then speed up to the actual **tempo** of the song.

Experiment with staying on the same bass note when the guitar changes chords. If the note goes with both chords, it can sound great. Even a third chord often works. Now reverse it—have the guitar stay on the same chord and change the bass note three times.

Next, play some two-note chords on the bass: Let one string ring out openly while pressing down notes on the string next to it. The open string ringing is called a **drone**.

Pay attention to the drums and work on being consistent in your meter. You can also practice with a metronome. It's like swinging two baseball bats but hitting with only one, or swimming with two bathing suits but racing with just one. Metronomes help you play with better time, which is a good goal.

Some people play with a pick in their right hand and some people play with the fingers of their right hand (reverse for lefties). As a beginner, a pick is usually the easier choice, as playing with your fingers can be like learning to drive a stick shift at the same time you are learning to drive. In the long run, though, being comfortable playing with your fingers is useful for versatility. In addition, finger playing can make a nicer, softer, more human sound, if that is what you're going for. Punk rock bass styles on one note played really fast are best played with a pick for greater speed and accuracy. Try to alternate between up and down strokes.

It is okay to make up your own way to play. Elizabeth Cotten taught herself to play guitar upside down and backward and invented an unprecedented and complex picking style to make this work for her. It sounds amazing and like no one else, but keep in mind that if you ever do want to play conventionally you will have some bad habits to unlearn.

To practice, play along with records or CDs, and pick out the bass part. Playing along is great practice and great fun; you feel like you're in the band. I learned this way. My favorite recommendations for entire records to do this with are *Faith* and *Seventeen Seconds,* two early, amazingly meditative records by the Cure. As you'll find out, there are lots of simple bass lines in modern rock music, as well as in old-time country and folk music. Simplicity = bliss.

When you first start playing bass, the tips of your fingers will be sore. You will just have to go through the hazing period until calluses develop. Persevere. Calluses rule, and must be kept up with a good dose of daily practice or you will have to build them up again.

A big part of enjoying bass playing is to Zen out on repetition. Get into your groove. Pour your feelings into one note or one simple part, over and over. Fall in love with your part and the feeling of locking in, and you can play bass forever.

I love playing the bass because it is loud, tough, and powerful, the glue of a band. Electric bass is a fusion of the harmony of a guitar and the rhythm of the drums. It is deep enough that the vibrations can crawl through my skin to my bones and reverberate there, in the center.

Being in a band is one of the most fulfilling aspects of my life. I play music with other people because music creates a bridge from one person to another, through sound and intention.

Shannon O'Brien

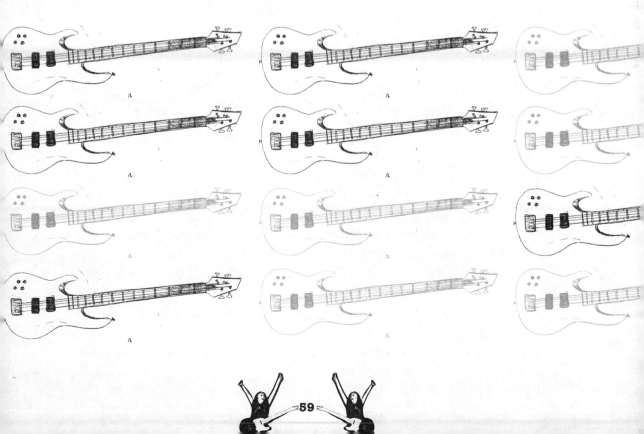

Finding THE Elusive ONE:
HOW to PLAY The DRUMS

BY STS

Every culture and every genre of music has different ways of banging on something to beat out the rhythm of a song. There are drums designed for orchestras, marching bands, and electronic music. Latin and salsa music feature timbales, the traditional music of India uses tablas, and rock music most often employs the drum set.

If you are an aspiring drummer, there are a million ways to play a drum set. You can bang around all over every part of a kit, tap everything lightly, make up patterns that have a rhythm you like, even hit the side of a hubcap balanced on top of a cymbal stand. But to get serious about keeping rhythm, you must find the "one."

The one, sometimes called the downbeat, is the first note of the measure. Turn on a good song and start bobbing your head, moving your feet, tapping your fingers, or clapping, and most likely, you've found the one. The one makes you dance.

The reason you're dancing is that everyone in the band knows when every measure starts, and they can find it over and over again, and it creates an irresistible pulse. In a rock band, this is because the drumbeat is on time, and the drummer is pounding out a steady rhythm that everyone in the band can follow. The drummer holds the one close to her heart, and shares it with the rest of her band. For most bands, it doesn't work right if someone else in the band is deciding the rhythm and tempo for the song. When the drummer counts off "One! Two! Three! Four!" she is exclaiming to the band where the one is, how long the measure is, and the tempo of the song.

The One Epiphany

To witness the mystery of how to make that dance beat happen, sit down behind a drum set. (If you are left-handed, you can either reverse the following directions to suit using your dominant left hand to keep time, or you can try out your ambidextrous skills and see if playing right-handed is possible for you.)

First, put your left foot on the high-hat pedal so the cymbals are pressed together. Pick up your drumsticks, and position your right drumstick over the closed high-hat cymbals. Now hit the high hat with your right stick while saying, out loud, in a steady, clocklike fashion:

One! And! Two! And! Three! And! Four! And!

Without pausing or sounding like a galloping horse, do this four times in a row. If you hit your high hat while counting along out loud, and didn't skip a beat or pause between the last "And!" and the next "One!" you have found the one—four times in a row! The beginning of the measure! w00t! Most rock music uses this timing. It's called four-four, or 4/4. Turn on the radio and see if you can count through part of a song using this 4/4 counting technique.

Being able to find the one might be hard at first. Even though I couldn't clap along in time to "This Land Is Your Land" at the school assembly (great shame, there), I absolutely *knew* I wanted to be a drummer. No rhythm skills paired with a small sparkly red drum set in the garage equals the fact that it took me two weeks to find the one and play my first rock beat. So hang in there. Seriously, I can now clap the heck out of a backbeat to a "This Land" remix.

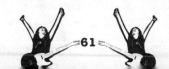

If you play in a band, you will notice your bass player start rocking her head to the beat. Your guitarist will start tapping her foot, or concentrating deeply on her chord progression. Finding the one and sharing it with your band is a huge first-time discovery and feels better than anything else in the world. The only way to truly find the one is to practice playing any of the following drumbeats over and over and over and over.

Basic Rock Beat, Extraordinarily Basic Notation

Drum notation is a way of teaching a drum beat and writing down a drumbeat so you can remember it. What follows is a lesson in the basic rock beat, in the style of notation commonly used at Rock Camp to teach new beats to beginning drummers.

The symbol for the high-hat cymbal is ✕.

Every time an ✕ ✕ ✕ ✕ ✕✕ ✕✕ comes up, hit the high hat and say the number and "+" symbol above it, just like in the exercise below. Hitting the high hat and counting out loud is written in very basic drum notation like this:

4/4 beat (high hat only)

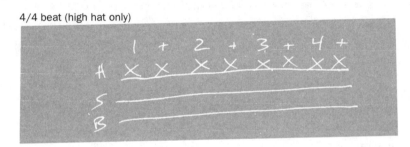

Read the notes from left to right. The top line is for the high hat. The second line is for the snare drum, and the bottom line is for the bass drum. Some people write an X for the high hat, snare, and bass notes. I use music notes for snare and bass. You can use a smiley face if you want. It doesn't matter what it looks like, as long as you hit the thing you're supposed to hit when it's written in the notation. Try this: Hit the bass drum using your right foot on the kick-drum pedal, hit the high hat with your right stick and say "One!" out loud, at the same time. That is the first bit of the "rock beat," and it looks like this:

4/4 beat (bass drum on one with high hat)

Repeat, in a steady, clocklike manner (clocks keep time, too) four times. Keep practicing until you can consistently hit the bass drum and the high hat together on one. Next, try playing your snare drum with your left hand (positioned comfortably *under* your right hand) when you say "Two!" At this time, only hit the high hat and snare. Do not hit the bass drum on two. Can you play this beat?

4/4 beat (snare on two with high hat)

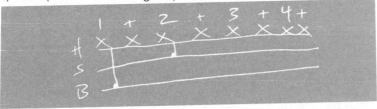

Can you do this beat four times in a row and hit the high hat and snare on two every time?

Once you've gotten the hang of hitting the bass and high hat together at the beginning of the measure, and then the snare and high hat together on the two, you're ready for the rest of the rock beat. Play this beat really, really slow. Like waiting-in-the-doctor's-office-with-your-mom slow. Or waiting-for-Harry-Potter-Book-7-to-come-out slow. Like-you-might-die-of-boredom slow. Try to hit all the notes as written below. Whenever you say "And," only hit the high hat.

4/4 Basic Rock Beat

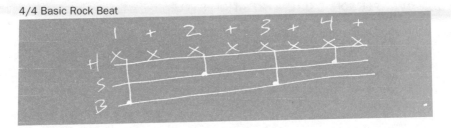

Did you hit the high hat by itself when you said "And"? Did you hit the high hat and snare together on "two" and "four"? Did you go so slow you forgot you were playing the drums between notes? This is *one measure of a basic rock beat.* Go back and try it again. If you've got this pattern down, try playing not-as-slow as before. Repeat to your heart's content. As I mentioned previously, it took two weeks for my brain to comprehend three-limb independence (that's what you're doing when you play this beat), and create the new neural pathways (true!) required of such an accomplishment. In the end, like brushing your teeth with the opposite hand, drumming makes you smarter. It's like a massive mental exercise and you gotta practice to get good at it!

One trick to playing the drums is "forgetting" your right hand is playing the high hat so it just goes automatically at the tempo you want. This frees up your brain to concentrate on what your right foot is doing on the bass drum and what your left hand is doing on the snare drum. Keep your high hat going *no matter what,* even if you mess up the other drums. Try playing a beat and thinking about anything but the high hat. Or, just keep practicing. Eventually, your hand will go on its own and you won't have to concentrate so hard.

STANDARD DRUM NOTATION

Yes, there is a standard, formal way to write drum notation, but you don't have to be able to read and write *their* way in order to play drums. It's usually required for you to learn standard drum notation and be able to read music efficiently if you want to join the drum corps or orchestra. If your brain accepts standard notation, generations of drummers have documented millions of beats, at least forty drum rudiments, and even tabbed out Sleater-Kinney's first 10-inch, and this is all available online, in drummer magazines, and in countless books on playing the drums.

If standard drum notation is not for you, you can become a drummer who learns by listening and making up her own style of notation, or avoid writing anything down altogether and make a recording of your beat.

YOUR OWN PERSONAL DRUM NOTATION STYLE

For years, I used notation that looked like this.

• — • • —

Believe it or not, the dots were bass, the dashes were snare, and you read it like a poem, taking pauses as they were written in the line. This notation was often accompanied by notes like "Batman part" or "Slow Enya Jammy Thing." Using this admittedly vague and barely recognizable drum notation style was not only untraditional; it wasn't very useful for anyone but me. But I needed to remember my drumbeats, I didn't know notation, and it pulled me through many years of writing drumbeats in hundreds of songs with several bands. If you want, make up your own style.

The most important thing is, when you come up with anything on the drums you like, find a way to remember it that works for you. Even if you've just written the most

amazing beat and you're sure it's burned into your memory, jot something down just in case. (Or record it, if you happen to be set up for recording, but you might have trouble in playback telling what each body part is doing.) There's no correct way for you to write down and remember your drumbeat, no matter what anyone may say.

More Drum Beats!

The trick to learning these drumbeats is to play them *s-l-o-w-l-y* the first few times through. If you can play a beat all the way through without messing up or speeding up, you're ready to try playing it faster. Once you've got a few beats down, you're ready to make up your own. Try learning these beats, and then move on to experimenting and writing beats that sound good to you. Keep track of the one and keep your friends, family, pets, and bandmates dancing!

4/4 Rock Beat

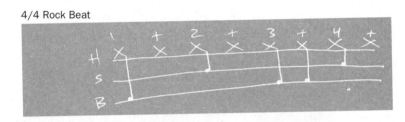

4/4 Surf Style

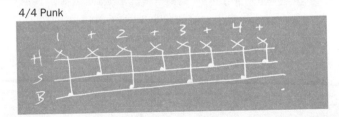

4/4 Punk

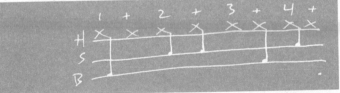

4/4 Rock Beat Variation

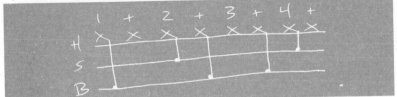

How TO KEEP YOUR DRUMMER HAPPy

by sts

1. Set up in a circle and adjust your levels so everyone can hear each other.

▶▶ Make all amps face the drummer, and put small amps on chairs to get the speakers at the drummer's ear level. Tip big amps a few inches backward by leaning them against a wall or placing a book underneath to raise the angle.

▶▶ Everyone should be able to see each other playing. If your drummer usually keeps time but for some reason is off, she probably can't hear enough of whichever instrument she needs to hear the most, usually something in the rhythm section. Try turning up the bass, rhythm guitar, or keys (or turning things down) until she's comfortable.

2. Have good feng shui in the practice space.

▶▶ Wrap up and put away all unnecessary cords.

▶▶ Put away all unused equipment (mic stands, amps, instruments).

▶▶ Make sure that everyone has as much comfortable space to stand in a circle as possible.

3. Keep your drummer involved.

▶▶ There are times when the stringed instruments need to work things out together. Try to break the song down into smaller parts (verse, chorus, bridge, breakdown) so that the drummer can put drums to one part at a time.

▶▶ Don't spend more than ten minutes on a single part. If you need more than that, try to simplify the part so the drummer can join in as soon as possible.

▶▶ Let the drummer make suggestions by asking her things like, "How does that sound to you?" "Should we go faster or slower?" "Should we play loud or quiet here?" etc.

▶▶ If you think the stringed instruments are going to take a while to figure out HOW to play the part everyone has decided to play, let the drummer know by saying "Is it okay if we take five or ten minutes to figure this out?" or "Do you mind waiting while we try to work out this part?"

➡ Show the drummer what chord(s) you are playing at problem areas, such as transitions between verse and chorus, so she can cue from what they look like visually. You can give other cues for upcoming changes such as a nod, a kick, a dip in the guitar or bass, or a scary look.

4. If you're taking too much time to work out a part and your drummer is bored:

➡ Stringed instruments should go somewhere else to work on a part, and let the drummer play on the drums in the practice space.

➡ Postpone working on difficult melodic parts for a practice that is scheduled where the drummer does not have to attend.

➡ Ask your drummer if she's cool with giving you the time you need to work out your part. If she wants to move on, then move on and work on the part later.

5. If your band has spent more than fifteen minutes working on a part without the drummer, find a way to incorporate the drummer immediately.

➡ SIMPLIFY the part so the drummer can start playing with the band.

➡ Go back to an easier part the drummer already knows.

➡ Take a break to THRASH, MAKE NOISE, or write a thirty-second song.

6. HAVE FUN TOGETHER! If the vibe is too stressful:

➡ Take a break.

➡ Write a fast fun song. Maybe this is the *real* song your band wants to write!

➡ Check in on how everyone is feeling.

7. Give your drummer lots of love.

ThE KEYBOARD iS KeY

BY AMY SABIN

Imagine you could change the sound of your voice anytime you like—make it high or low, harsh or soothing. Imagine the ability to make your voice imitate all sorts of instruments. Well, you *can* do that with a keyboard. Keyboards allow you to access countless voices or tones and manipulate them to get your own sound. Keyboards look deceivingly like small, plastic pianos with electric cords attached, but they are really so much more.

Why You're Going to Love Playing Keyboards

▶▶ Keyboards can sound like pianos, but you don't need to hire a piano mover to take them anywhere you please.

▶▶ You can play the lead and the rhythm. Keyboard riffs have been the building blocks for many great rock songs.

▶▶ Your keyboard can sound like any instrument in the band. Guitar, bass, drums, and plenty of other instruments. When your bandmates yell, "Drum solo!" you can yell, "Do you mean me or the *other* drummer?"

▶▶ You can use both hands, but you don't have to! Use one hand, or just one finger if you feel like it. Your other hand can dance, make a fist to pump or wave around in the air, hang at your side, or push buttons and move knobs and levers. Or forget your hands completely: You can play with your knees, toes, elbows, and/or shoulders, if you want to.

▶▶ Stand up, sit down, dance around—what's your pleasure? As a keyboardist you have the freedom to do all of these things while you play. And for those of you who like the idea of running around on stage carrying your instrument and doing that well-recognized, signature guitar dip, there is a keyboard for you: it's called a Keytar (get it?). See 1980s music videos for reference!

▶▶ When you have a keyboard in front of you, it's simply a matter of finding the mood or sound you want to get out there. The almost never-ending choices can range anywhere from chiming, high, pretty tones to low, loud, bass-like tones to tones nobody has ever heard before, depending on the type of keyboard.

All Kinds of Keyboards

Now that we've confirmed that you can truly rock a keyboard, the questions are where to get one and which one to get. You don't have to spend a lot of money to get something great. Look in places that sell used instruments: thrift stores, pawnshops, and shops that specialize in second-hand musical gear. Music stores that carry new instruments are also good places to look and try out many different kinds of keyboards.

Also—and this is important!—try it before you buy it. Don't be shy about spending time playing all the keyboards on display at the music store. Look for a keyboard with plenty of tones that you like. If you want to know more about the options out there, check out the book *Vintage Synthesizers* by Mark Vail.

Keyboards work in many different ways, so open the manual for your keyboard and read up on how to get all the different sounds. If you get a used and/or vintage keyboard without a manual, do an Internet search under the brand name and model number of your keyboard to find one.

Accessorize!

So, you've got a keyboard picked out that you love, but you'll need two other items before you're ready to rock out.

AMPLIFIER

While some keyboards come with built-in speakers, a good amp is a must if you want to play with other people or be truly loud on your own. There are lots of options for keyboard amps out there. Some are made specifically for keyboards, but you can also use amps meant for other instruments. You may find that amps made for keys tend to work a little better when it comes to making sure that you don't get drowned out by the other instruments.

When in doubt, go ahead and ask the salesperson at the music store for advice. Ignore sales pressure, test as many as you like (preferably with your own keyboard), and go with your gut. It's a good idea not to buy either the most expensive option or the cheapest. Usually something in the middle range will be your best bet. And don't forget to buy a ¼-inch cord, a.k.a instrument cord, to connect your keyboard to the amp.

STAND

You also need a stand for your keyboard to sit on; they are very hard to balance on your knees or sling over a shoulder.

Get to Know Your Keys

The general rule of thumb with keyboards is: the buttons are there to be pushed and the knobs are there to be turned!! Experiment, experiment, experiment! Also, every single key is your friend. If you hit a wrong note, the right one is just a short distance away. And besides, sometimes "wrong" notes can be very cool. Try out every sound; figure out which ones make the most sense to you. While playing alone or along with a bandmate, feel free to change your tone until you find the one that moves you or expresses what you feel about the song. You are the biggest expert on what sounds good.

You might hear seasoned keyboardists refer to something called "presets." Presets are the tones that come built in to your keyboard. You choose one from the many sound options (piano, strings, outer space) to start playing; if you don't like it as you play or find it's not right for the song, choose another by pressing a button. With some types of keyboards, you can modify tones or create your very own sound. You can also use amps or distortion pedals to modify preset tones.

Starting to Play

READING MUSIC OR PLAYING BY EAR

You don't have to know music theory or be able to read music to be a good keyboardist. Some people find music theory extremely helpful, even necessary, and some people learn just enough to communicate with their fellow musicians.

The truth is, there are plenty of people out there who don't and can't read music notes on paper who write terrific songs. There are some people who feel that it's extremely important to know how to read music, and others who learn how to read it and then promptly choose to forget. There are musicians who have no use for music theory and others who use it every day! The great thing is that you get to decide for yourself.

It's a good idea to learn the names of keys, so that you can communicate with the other people in your band. For example, your guitarist shows you a song she wrote and proceeds to tell you that this song starts in a C chord then goes to a G chord, etc. If it's hard to remember the names, just put a piece of tape with the note name on the key. This is what the names of your keys are:

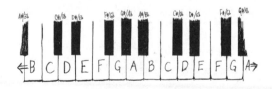

This basic knowledge can help a lot with beginning to locate the notes you need for a chord in a song. Or, you can just listen to the song and use your ear to find the notes you like. Learning music is like learning a language, and before you learned to read and write, you could already express yourself out loud. Likewise, you can express yourself musically without knowing how to read or write notes. If you find music theory intimidating but you like the idea of learning it eventually, it might be easier to learn to "speak" with your instrument first.

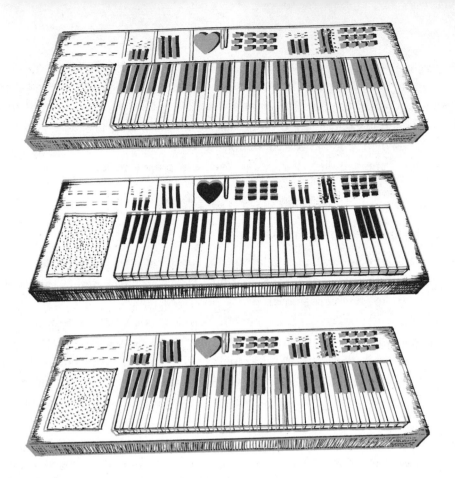

WRITING PARTS

After you have explored your keyboard and identified which sounds you like, you're ready to write keyboard parts! Here are three basic building blocks to work with:

Single notes—String single notes together into a melody or a riff.
Chords—Play two, three, or more notes simultaneously.
Arpeggios—Play three-or-more-note chords one note at a time in a pattern of your choosing.

Make up different parts by using these techniques in combination. Use your ear to find notes you think sound good. Ask your guitar player what chord she's playing and play the note with the same name on your keyboard.

You can also use your keys to play sound effects, which create or expand the mood of the music coming from your bandmates. Another good thing to try is to imitate vocal or instrument melodies to songs that you like. This can help give you an idea of the layout of the keyboard, and you may at some point find yourself modifying a favorite tune and making it your own.

Trust Yourself

A good thing to remember for any instrument is that what you play doesn't have to be complicated to be good. While there are lots of black and white keys on your keyboard and infinite combinations of notes, preset sounds, and effects you can use, don't get overwhelmed or intimidated, because even the simplest part on a keyboard can be dramatic and beautiful. Even one note, long or short, loud or quiet, played with conviction can be the key that unlocks a song! Some of the greatest songs out there are made up of two or three chords or a few simple notes in a catchy riff. When you're sitting at your keyboard, let your fingers do the walking, let your ear be your guide, and trust yourself.

Using SAMPLeRS, KEYS, anD BEAT Machines to Comp0se

BY MIREAYA MEDINA

Composing music using electronic instruments is fun, fairly simple, and versatile. First, I would like to dispel some common myths about beat machines, samplers, and synthesizers. People often think that drum machines are only useful for monotonous hip-hop songs or annoying techno. The truth is, drum machines can be used in any way for any genre of music. Samplers have the same stigma. Sampling does not mean that you are ripping off a "real musician's" hooks or riffs. Samplers are instruments that can be used to create sounds that are owned by their creator.

Make a Beat

I start by using a drum machine to create a rhythm. A drum machine is a plastic box or module containing sampled percussion sounds and a sequencer, which is a little electronic brain that records and remembers the pattern information you program into it. The sequencer takes multiple samples and arranges them in an organized time pattern according to how you program it. After you pick the sound or sounds you like from the collection, or "bank," of prerecorded sounds in the machine, you can choose your time signature, tempo, and pattern length and record a pattern. Most newer drum machines have a screen that tells you the number of bars, the beats per minute, or BPM, and other information about the sounds and patterns you're working with.

The difference between a drum machine and a sampler is that a sampler lets you record external sounds and sequence them, and a drum machine only allows you to arrange the sounds it comes with. The sounds in a drum machine are assigned to several rubber pads (kind of like a really big telephone keypad). To make, or trigger, sounds, you have to press the pads.

Before you start to record a pattern:
1. Find the drum sounds you like—bass, snare, cowbell, cricket, whatever.
2. Choose the length of your pattern. Length is usually expressed in bars. A common length would be four bars.
3. Choose the speed of your pattern. This is expressed as BPM, and indicates the tempo of the pattern you've recorded.
4. Choose whether you want to Quantize. When the Quantize function is on, the rhythm stays absolutely steady, like a metronome. If your pattern has any slight slow downs or speed ups, Quantizing alters it to match the beat exactly. The Quantize function also tells your sequencer to sync up every pattern to a designated beat count.

Record a Pattern

Now the fun begins.

Before you press Record, make sure that the metronome is turned on. This will help you keep track of where to add sounds, where to edit sounds, or where to delete them entirely.

Press Record and play your beat on the pads. There's your drum track!

(Turning the Quantize function on will correct any rhythm that is a little "off." I don't use Quantize very often because I like the beat to have a human touch and an organic sound.)

Now it's time to add the bass! Some drum machines have bass that can be added in the same manner that beats are created. In my opinion, bass is everything. Bass placement can make a song really good, or really bad. When adding bass, I usually use keyboard sounds that are deep and have a strong vibration.

Creating a great beat takes time. I keep track of which notes I am using, so that if I want to add more notes they won't clash or result in a muddy sound. I try not to get annoyed if I have to re-record a high-hat sound more than twenty times before I am satisfied.

Sampling

Sampling is one of my favorite techniques to use and is relatively easy. Think of a sampler as a drum machine that doesn't have sounds already in it—you have to put the sounds in yourself. Some terminology is important to note when using a sampler. (Note that not all devices use the same terms; read your user's manual to get acquainted with your machine's terms and features.) Samplers are pretty intuitive, but it is still good to know what is happening when certain functions are selected.

Sample: A digital recording of a particular sound or sounds.

Loop: A sample that replays repeatedly at a set rate/tempo/BPM.

Gate: When the Gate function is engaged, your sample will play only while the pad is being pressed.

Trigger: A funciton for playing the entire sample from beginning to end one time, without looping.

Reverse: A feature that reverses the playback of a sample, that is, plays it backward (my personal favorite).

Lo-fi: A feature that plays samples in low fidelity, for a sound that is old and crackly, in a good way.

Stereo: A function that assigns your audio signals to the left and right channels.

To me, sampling is an art form all its own because *anything* can be sampled! Sampling adds so much texture to my songs. I can make a background texture of my big brother snoring, my cat meowing, a construction site in my neighborhood, or my grandmother

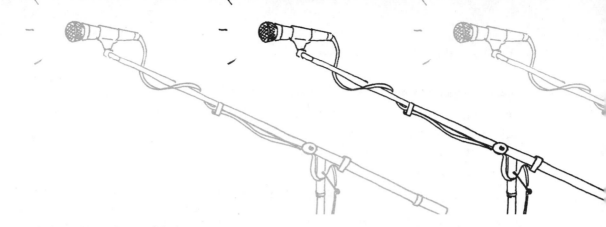

ragging about the world. When coming up with samples, I keep in mind what kind of feeling I am trying to evoke in the song as a whole.

A sad love song might need some slow, dramatic strings. I will use notes that harmonize with my bass line. I am also aware of the beats per minute so that all of the sounds will synchronize when I am finished. For example, if the beat pattern is 120 beats per minute, I record a sample at 120 BPM, 60 BPM, or 30 BPM. Occasionally, the BPM may not match numerically but will still create a compatible sound. This is true especially when using the Reverse function to loop samples.

Recording a Sample

To record a sample from an electronic source like a keyboard, guitar, bass, or CD player, I use a direct plug-in to the device. First I find the output of the instrument that I am sampling from, then I use a ¼" cable to plug it into the Microphone In jack on the sampler. If an instrument doesn't have an output, I will use the Headphone Out jack. (Again, not all samplers have the same names for their Inputs and Outputs; you might see Microphone Input, Line Input, or both.)

It is very important to check the volume level on the instrument being sampled and on the sampler itself before starting to record. Samples can become distorted if the recording volume is too loud, or, if a sample is not loud enough, the other instruments in the song will drown it out. I use headphones so that I can make sure that the recording level is not peaking too much.

Sometimes it helps to record the sample while listening to the drum machine so that I can play at the right tempo. When I record vocals or acoustic instruments, I use a microphone. Even if your sampler has a microphone built in, I suggest using a plug-in mic to cut down on outside noises getting picked up while recording. I am always aware of the volume of every instrument that is being used and how the volume level determines what is being picked up by the microphone.

After I have recorded a sample, I listen to how it syncs up with the beat. If I don't like the way that it sounds, I can fix it.

To change the speed of the sample, during playback I mark the start point and the end point of the part that I want to keep. Then I "truncate," which means that I delete the unwanted portions of the sample. Once I've done that, I can change the BPM of the sample.

Keyboards

After I have recorded the samples for the song that I am producing, I start working on my keyboard hooks. Using a variety of sounds is crucial for textural layering purposes. If the samples and drum machine bass are in a deep or mid range, the keyboard sound should be in an upper-mid to high range.

Playing the keyboard helps me come up with lyrics and vocal harmonies. I listen to what the song is saying to me. Sometimes I hear words in the keyboard parts, other times I have thoughts that the music is conjuring up. This might sound a little weird, but I can honestly say that the music itself creates my lyrics and I just sing them.

I have a lyric book where I write ideas when they arise. I record songs I'm writing on a little tape deck and play it back. While I listen to the music composition as a whole, I sing along. Writing lyrics can take a very long time or no time at all. I make sure to write it all down in my songwriting journal.

Vocals

Once I have the lyrics down, I start trying different vocal effects by running my microphone cord through a guitar effects processor or pedal. The really cool thing about using guitar effects is that I have control of the mix, sound, and the kind of effect that I am aiming for.

I plug the microphone into the effects processor **input** and run a ¼" cable from the processor output into a vocal amp or PA. I like the dramatic sounds of my vocals when I use effects. I don't feel like I have to use them, but I choose to.

Remember, you can use all of the music experience that is inside of you to create something all your own!

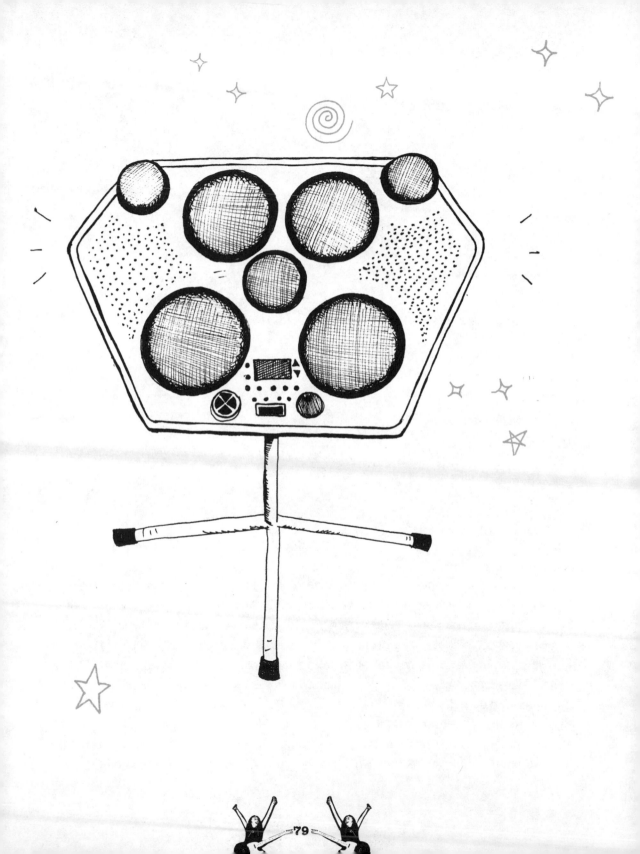

PUTTING it ALL together

BY KATE WALSH AND MARISA ANDERSON

So, you've figured out how to play some notes and chords on your guitar or bass. Maybe you have a drummer and a keyboardist who want to come play with you. You're finding your voice, and maybe you've got some lyrics in progress. You rock! But how do you put it all together and get started? Truly, physically, nuts-and-boltsy? Here are some guidelines to follow from your bedroom or the privacy of your head to your practice space and a group situation; to help you go from silence to noise to organized sound.

Remember: It's natural to feel shy the first time you get together to play music with other people. Don't rush it. Take some time to get to know each other. Hang out, talk about where you're from, what school you go to, what music you listen to, what kind of song you want to write (fast, slow, melodic, thrashy, with lyrics or instrumental, etc.). Get comfortable with each other and then get started with the music.

Writing music can start with a beat, a guitar or bass pattern, or a melody played on the keys or sung out loud. At this stage it is EXTREMELY IMPORTANT to not judge yourself or each other. Let the music happen without thinking too critically about it—that can come later.

So call a meeting! Find a room that meets your volume and equipment needs (do you want to plug in or just play acoustic?), set the time and date, call around to confirm the day before or morning of, gather your gear, and get over there.

Get in Tune

First things first—Get in tune. The keyboard is in a standardized tuning, and the guitar and bass need to be in tune with it and with each other, or your band is going to sound pretty weird. (Note: Occasionally a keyboard will get out of whack, and some come with a pitch control knob that can be turned to another world of tuning, so if something seems really weird with a keyboard, check it against a tuner and check to make sure the pitch control knob, if present, is at zero.)

Use a tuner to save yourselves time and trouble. Make sure the battery has juice (keep fresh ones stashed), then plug one end of an instrument cable into the jack on your guitar and the other end into the Input jack of the tuner. Following the manufacturer's instructions, read the needle or digital light to tune each string as follows, from lowest (thickest, and closest to your head) to highest (thinnest, closest to the floor):

Guitar = EADGBE

Bass = EADG

TUNING DRUMS

You may be surprised to hear that drums need tuning, too. There are a few basic checks to attend to for any drum to sound good. If you think the drums sound dull or too thuddy, or the heads are really loose, tighten them up using a drum key—a small, T-shaped metal tool with a hollow bit that fits over the lugs (the square bolts holding the drum head down) on the drum hardware around the rim of the drum. Always tighten the lugs in a star pattern, $^{3}\!\!\underset{5}{\bigstar}\!\!^{4}_{2}$, not a circle. Tap the edges of the drum all the way around; if each tap sounds the same and the drumhead is tight and resonant, you're in tune.

Get in the Groove

Once you're set up and tuned, follow the next steps in any order. Any instrument or voice can start it off.

ESTABLISH A BEAT.

When it's time to play music, ask the drummer to play a beat—any beat—and have the guitar, bass, or keyboard player make noise in time with the beat. Everyone can also join in, keeping the beat by clapping or banging along at first. If your drummer isn't ready to just jump in, the guitar or bass player can start first.

EVERYONE MAKE SOUND/NOISE/MUSIC.

Once the drummer has found her beat, the guitar, bass, and keyboard player can start following, with whatever they want—chords, single notes, noisy distorted chaos, a melody line, etc. The bass player can play along with the notes of the guitar and the beat of the drums, or play a repeated pattern that sounds good to her. The keyboard player can use her ears to follow the bass player and play the bass note, follow the guitar player and play the chord, or find a cool riff and repeat it.

Don't worry about being "right" while you're finding your part! You can play notes in any order. You can play notes that are not in the chord or play out of rhythm—it could work. . . . Be creative, and decide for yourself if what you're playing sounds good.

COMPLETE ONE PART AND CREATE ANOTHER ONE.

Once you have a part that everybody feels good about playing, you may find the momentum leads to writing more. Try to develop two basic ideas and practice switching back and forth between them.

THE MUSIC IS GOING REALLY WELL, BUT WHERE DO WE GET WORDS?

General brainstorm. Get in a circle and write anything that comes to mind. Cut and paste phrases together randomly, according to what sounds good or feels good. Don't worry about lyrics making sense.

Brainstorm around a specific topic. Pick a theme and talk about it, let your ideas and random references fly. Again, the lyrics don't have to make sense.

Exquisite-corpse-style lyric writing. One person writes a line on a piece of paper and passes it on to the next person, who reads the first line and adds one of her own, then passes it on. Continue passing and writing until you have enough words for a song.

Sometimes you just need a little space . . . Send every bandmember into her own corner or space for ten minutes to come up with some words. Come back together, share what you have written, and see how you can weave bits together.

OKAY, I HAVE SOME WORDS I'M READY TO SING—YIKES! HOW DO I GET A SONG TO COME OUT?

It's important for the singer to have something to practice while the band is practicing the music. If your vocalist is shy about just opening her mouth and belting it out, she can start by speaking the words over the music. Lots of songs start with one sentence or idea repeated, spoken or sung, over the music.

If someone has written a melody or vocal line, it can be fun to sing it together.

AWESOME, WE'VE GOT A VERSE, WITH WORDS AND EVERYTHING! UHHHH, NOW WHAT? OH—A CHORUS!

When you're looking to move from your verse to the chorus, a good rule of thumb is to keep it simple—Change one thing. Maybe the beat, or the chords, or the delivery. Then change another thing, perhaps adding or subtracting effects. That may easily be all the change you need for the music. For the words, try repeating an important vocal line a few times in a row. Everybody yell! Everybody whisper. Put a sudden stop right before the chorus, and then hit it big, all together, all at once. There are infinite ways to make the chorus stand out. Practice going between the verse and the chorus until everybody is comfortable.

WORD, WE'VE GOT A CHORUS, TOO! I THINK A BRIDGE WOULD BE RAD!

Bridges are awesome (see page 40). A bridge may be a beautiful section in the middle of a song that connects ideas. It may also be totally random—everybody start clapping and singing. Everyone freak out! Not every song needs a bridge, and bridges can be quiet little breaks in the action, but if your band wants to be out of control for a while, the bridge is one place to do it.

WOW . . . THIS SONG IS SO GOOD—IF ONLY IT HAD A SOLO!

Soloing can be awesome—or not. If it sounds fun and feels good, go for it. The band can play the chorus or the verse while the singer takes a break, and whoever is

soloing plays their instrument. Make sure if you are soloing that your volume is turned up, or the band comes down in volume a little bit. This is your moment to be heard! The band can drop out while the drummer plays a mad solo, too.

WE HAVE ALL THE PARTS NOW, BUT WE'RE HAVING TROUBLE PUTTING IT ALL TOGETHER.

Now that the song is written, it's time to arrange it. Communication is key here! Once the song is underway, it can be tricky knowing when to switch between the verse, the chorus, and the bridge. Label the different parts (intro, outro, weird part, verse, chorus, bridge, random freakout, etc.), so that everyone is calling them the same name, and write them down so you can all refer to the same chart. For example, if the guitar is playing four counts of Em and four counts of A7, and going back and forth three times, you can write it down like this:

```
Em Em Em Em
A7 A7 A7 A7
3x
and count like this:
1& 2& 3& 4&
1& 2& 3& 4&
```

The bass and keys players can follow this chart by playing the root notes (E and A) and building a line based on these notes. Everyone should try to keep track of the 1 count. If you get lost, count out loud together while you play.

Make sure everybody is looking at each other; this means you have to look up from your instrument often! Identify specific cues for the transitions between parts, listen to each other, and work together. Once you're rock solid getting through the parts in the order you wrote down, talk about the arrangement; you may want to add a verse, double a chorus, or move the bridge to a different spot, depending on how the song feels when you play it as a whole. Does it get boring at any point, or end too soon! Is the the intro long enough, do all the instruments need to come in at once or should they come in one at a time? These are just some of the questions to ask yourself about the arrangement of your song.

Practice Practice Practice!

PLAY THE SONG. A *LOT*.

Practice changing smoothly between all the parts. If a particular transition is causing trouble, practice going into it and out of it until it feels comfortable. Work toward memorizing the song.

FIGURE OUT DYNAMIC CHANGES.

One of the most satisfying things about working as a band is deciding on the dynamics of your song, which includes everything from volume level to the sort of journey a song takes you and the listener on. Get quiet, get loud, follow the song into its emotional extreme—don't hold back. Decide on instrumentation. Is this song going to start spare and quiet and build to a screaming crescendo, or is it going to start loud and have an amazing extended psychedelic breakdown? You can orchestrate these effects by using one voice or instrument in a section of the song and then adding gradually to full band, or decide on some volume cues to use as a group.

REMEMBER TO TAKE BREAKS!

Stay focused when it is time to stay focused, work hard, and then forget about it— really, just walk away. If you get bored or frustrated, maybe it's time to get some water, take a walk, stretch, or play a different song.

The most important thing is: Listen to each other and have fun!

So many buttons, so little time! Luckily, with the right vocabulary and a few basic concepts, you can demystify almost any piece of equipment. Once you know how to use your instrument to make a sound you like, you are ready to learn how to broadcast that sound far and wide.

In this chapter we cover the technical side of music making. Whether you're playing a live show or recording your band, you've got to know what the gear is called, how to use it, and what to do if it's not working.

Getting
HEARD:
how to
Set up
a PA

BY AMANDA PAULK

When you play your guitar, keyboard, or bass or belt out the lyrics you just wrote, that sound goes on quite a journey after leaving your lips or fingertips on its way to your audience's ears. After reading this section you'll understand where the sound goes and how to set up and operate a simple sound system.

When you sing, the sound of your voice is picked up by the microphone. The generic or shorthand term for this kind of microphone is vocal mic (pronounced "mike"). Sometimes it's referred to as "omni" or "cardio"—names based on the patterns of where these types of mics are most sensitive to sound (see page 92 for more on mic types).

If you are playing electric guitar, you need to plug into a guitar amp. An amp, or amplifier, is a device made to pick up a small sound and make it big. There are amps made specifically to transform the hum and twang of guitar strings into the riffs that make your teeth chatter, and there are amps for other instruments. What we think of as a guitar amp actually comprises an amp, a speaker, and certain elements of a mixer rolled into one or two pieces of equipment. Sometimes an amp isn't loud enough for everyone in the room to hear, and so that amp gets its own microphone. These microphones are referred to as instrument, or uni-directional, mics.

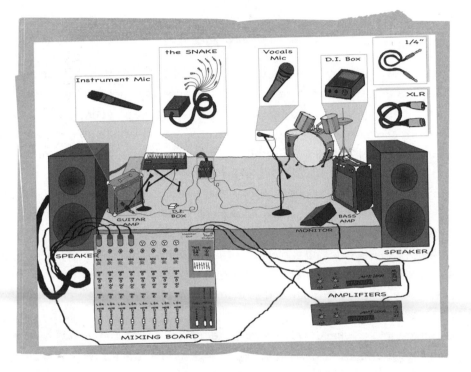

There are also special microphones designed just for drum sets, and there are even creative ways to use instrument microphones to mic a drum set, though it is not always necessary (unless you're recording), because unless you're in a REALLY big room, you can hear the drums pretty well.

Not every instrument can be amplified using microphones. Bass amps, keyboards, and acoustic guitars are generally not played into microphones (though nothing is impossible, and with good positioning anything can be mic'd). These instruments are generally run through a D.I. (direct input) box or a pre-amp. These devices are designed to regulate the sound coming from the instruments so that when it gets to the mixer it's equal in strength to the other inputs (vocal mics and instrument mics) on the stage.

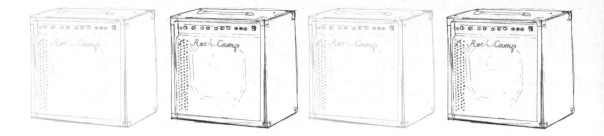

The Band

Once we've used microphones and D.I.s to pick up and transport sound from all our instruments, we need to make it all sound good together, and to do that, we use a piece of equipment called a **mixing console** (a.k.a. mixer, soundboard, board—the thing with all the knobs). The only problem is, the mixer is sometimes in the very back of the room and all our microphones are on the stage. Luckily there's a very handy thing called the **snake**. The snake works like an extension cord for some of the most commonly used cables. Every cord onstage plugs into a numbered input on the snake. The snake runs to the soundboard and plugs in to the matching inputs on the board.

A word about cords and cables: **XLR** (also called mic) cables or cords are generally used, as you may have guessed from their common name, for microphones. D.I. boxes usually have both XLR and ¼-inch inputs, of which either may be used. The ¼-inch cord (a.k.a. patch cord, instrument cable) is commonly used for plugging an instrument into an amp or D.I. box. Speaker cables, which sometimes have a ¼-inch connector, are made to carry a much stronger signal than a regular cable and are used to transport sound from the soundboard to the speakers. It's important to distinguish between speaker cables and instrument cables. Even though they often look exactly alike, they are intended for different purposes and carry very different electrical loads. Often, cords have writing on them to identify them as speaker or instrument cables. If not, label your cords yourself.

Each cord gets plugged into its own channel on the board. Each channel has a row of controls that only affect the instrument or microphone that is plugged into it. This means that you can change the pitch of the guitar with the **EQ** knobs, or turn up just the guitar in the monitors, even pan the sound to the left or right.

Near the top of the board is a knob marked **Gain**, which is designed to pick up more input signal (sound converted into electricity) the more you turn it up. Gain is useful for boosting a signal that is getting buried in the mix. (I think about Gain and

Volume like an iPod being played through a car stereo. When you turn up the volume on the iPod, that's like Gain—it increases the signal being sent to the stereo—and when you turn up the stereo, that's like Volume—it increases the amount of sound coming out of the speakers. If you get them balanced, you can make everything sound just right. See page 96 for more about Gain.) At the bottom of each channel is usually a slider or knob for volume, which determines how much sound is sent to the speakers.

Speakers

Once all the separate sounds from the different instruments and singers are mixed together on the board, the sound is ready to be sent to the speakers. Sound is sent as an electrical signal. At this point the signal is still pretty weak, only strong enough to be heard through headphones. Speakers are much larger and require more signal. To get this, we send the signal to a special amplifier called a power amp. Power amps make the signal strong enough for the speakers to turn it into sound that you hear.

Speakers that are turned toward the musicians are called "monitors" and speakers turned toward the audience are called "mains." The mix of sound that gets sent to the monitors is different than the mix of sound sent to the mains. Each channel has a place where it can be turned up or down in the monitors without affecting the main mix, so when someone on stage says, "Can I get a little more of her vocals in my monitor?" they are asking the soundperson to make the vocals louder in the onstage sound mix that only they are hearing.

Tips for Troubleshooting the Sound System

▶ *Check for juice:* Even the best among us can forget to turn on an amp or the board, so double-check that everything is plugged in and turned on.

▶ *Check all knobs and buttons:* Start out with every fader or volume knob all the way down and work systematically to turn each one up slowly, to avoid popping and feedback. Make sure the channel you are checking is turned up, and the Mute button is not on.

▶ *Check the lines:* Usually when something doesn't work it's just not going all the way from point A to point B. The first thing I do is check that the mic is plugged into the snake, the correct line from the snake is plugged into the correct channel

on the board, the board outputs go to the power-amp inputs, and the power-amp outputs to the speakers. Lots of sound systems don't include snakes. If this is the case, just check that the mics are plugged in to the correct channels on the mixing board.

▶▶ **Check the equipment:** Sometimes the problem is a bad cable. Try switching them out for ones you've tested and you know work.

YOUR GUIDE to MICROPHONES
by Beth Warshaw-Duncan

Microphones come in two main types: dynamic and condenser.

▶▶ Dynamic mics are more rugged and can be used with more instruments.

▶▶ Condenser mics are more sensitive and delicate.

Microphones are also classified by the direction and shape of the signal they pick up:

▶▶ *Cardioid* mics pick up sound from a heart-shaped area in front of the microphone (cardio = heart).

▶▶ *Omni-directional* mics pick up sound from every direction.

▶▶ *Uni-directional* mics (such as cardioid) pick up sound directly in front of them.

If you play drums:

▶▶ Kick drums take a dynamic directional mic.

▶▶ Snares take dynamic cardioid mics and require "close" miking.

▶▶ Toms and other drums take cardioids.

▶▶ Cymbals take a condenser mic.

▶▶ High hats take a small condenser mic.

▶▶ You will not need all these drum mics unless you are recording. In most rooms, drums can be heard very well without mics.

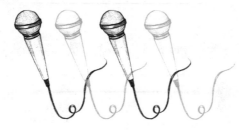

If you play bass:

➤ You can run your bass direct by plugging it into a direct box and then plugging the direct box into the appropriate channel of the mixer, or you can play through a bass amp that you can mic.

If you play keyboards, synthesizers, or organs:

➤ You can do the same as the bass—go direct, or mic your amp.

If you play electric guitar:

➤ You can also do what the bass and keys do and either mic your amp or run your guitar through a D.I. box. Generally, guitar players use an amp so that they can control their tone and overall sound. D.I. boxes are most often used for acoustic/electric guitars, that is, acoustic guitars that have been fitted with a pick-up so that they can be amplified. Lots of bass and guitar amps have a Line Out jack so that you can run a cord directly from the amp to the board.

➤ You might not need to run your bass or electric guitar through the board; a lot of amps are loud enough to be heard on their own.

If you play acoustic guitar:

➤ Use a dynamic mic and place it close to where the strings pass over the sound hole.

If you:

➤ play a stringed instrument like a violin or cello, place a dynamic mic close above the instrument. Violins and cellos can be outfitted with pick-ups as well.

➤ play a piano, use a pair of mics over the opened lid (if you can't lift the lid, angle a mic just above the keys).

➤ you sing, you can use whatever you think sounds best, usually a cardioid or omni mic.

AMPeD:

hOW DO I Get the Sound i Want?

BY MARISA ANDERSON

Amplifiers are not all created equally. Just like guitars, amps come in many styles, each with different possibilities for tone, volume, and effects. Amplifiers can be simple or they can sport a bewildering array of knobs and switches. Next to your hands and your guitar or bass, your amplifier is the most important component in the realization of your signature sound. Many guitar players spend years in their quest for the Holy Grail of good sound; that elusive and perfect combination of tone, volume, warmth, distortion, reverb, and other effects. Here's some background information to keep under your belt when you go to the music store to begin your search for the perfect amp.

The Basics

There are two main types of amplifiers: tube and solid state. Tube amps rely on vacuum tubes for their sound, like old-fashioned radios, and solid state amps rely on transistors. Tube amps are known for the warmth of their tone, while solid state amps are known for having a clean sound. Solid state amps are usually less expensive.

Amps also come in different sizes and relative volumes. How loud an amp is will be expressed in wattage, which is often written on the amp. For example, a Fender Bassman 100 has 100 watts, which is pretty loud for a guitar player, but not so loud for a bass player. Bass amps need higher wattage because they have bigger speakers.

(When picking an amp, make sure you can lift it. Unless you plan to only ever play at home, you will need to be able to move your amp in and out of cars, up and down stairs, and down long hallways. You can also get wheels installed on your amp to make moving it easier.)

When you approach an amp, the first thing you need to know is how to turn it on. On/off switches can usually be found either on the back or front right corner of the amp. Larger tube amps also have standby switches. The standby switch is located next to the on/off switch and must be turned on as well for the amp to power up. If your amp has a standby switch, it is best to turn on the amp and wait about five minutes before flipping the standby switch on. If you stop playing for a little while but know that you are coming back to play more, turn the standby switch off but leave the on/off switch on. The standby switch exists to protect the tubes from being blasted with too much electricity all at once.

What we call amplifiers are actually two different components: a) an *amp,* which receives the sound coming from the guitar, and b) the *speakers,* which broadcast that sound out into the world. When these components are in the same box, or *cabinet,* the amp is called a *combo* amp. When they are separate, the amp is called a "head," the speaker is called a "cabinet," and the two things together are sometimes referred to as a "stack." Don't worry if these terms are confusing—you can just call the whole thing an amp.

SPEAKERS

Speakers come in different sizes. The most common sizes are 10 inch, 12 inch, and 15 inch. These are usually just called 10s, 12s, or 15s. Each size has a slightly different tone and volume associated with it. Generally, the larger the speaker, the lower the sounds it is able to produce and the more volume it requires in order to be heard clearly. A speaker cabinet contains one or more actual speakers and is referred to by the number and size of speakers it contains. So, a 4x10 cabinet is a box containing 4 speakers, with each speaker being 10 inches in diameter. The more speakers you have, and the bigger the speakers, the louder you will be and the more

wattage your amp will need in order to push air through those speakers to make sound. Most speakers do not have an on/off switch—they are powered by the amp.

A combo amp will always have the right wattage for the speakers. If you are building a stack, you will need to pay attention to the electrical information written on the back of the amp and the back of the speaker. In very basic terms, you want the number of ohms and the number of watts to be the same on your amp head as they are on your speakers.

WHAT ARE ALL THESE KNOBS?

All amplifiers have volume controls. The simplest amps will have only one control for volume but most amps have a combination of knobs labeled Gain, Drive, or Pre as well as Volume or Level and Master Volume. These knobs are essential for dialing in the exact quality and volume of distortion in your sound.

The first amplifiers had only one volume control, which boosted the tiny electrical signal produced by a guitar so that it was "big" enough to hear and sent it out through the speaker. To control the loudness, you had to turn the volume knob up or down. When you turned it all the way up, you got distortion. When the knob was turned down you got clean tone.

That would have been fine except the only way to get distortion was to play really loud. What if you wanted a quiet distorted sound, or a loud clean sound? Guitar players started experimenting and came up with "Gain."

Gain can be called Pre or Drive, depending on your particular amp, and is often confused with Volume, but actually they are different. Remember when we talked about how amplifiers comprised two different components, the amp and the speakers? Well, when you plug your guitar into your amp, the cord sends an electrical signal from the pickups on your guitar to your amp. You then use the different knobs on the amp to modify the signal and send it on to the speakers, which convert the signal back into sound and play it out loud.

Gain controls the amount of signal being picked up and passed on to the speaker, and Volume controls the loudness of the sound that comes out of the speaker. When the signal being sent from the amp is bigger than what the speaker can handle, the result is distortion, a growly, fuzzy sound lots of people love.

Some amps have two volume knobs: Volume and Master Volume. Volume is meant to be used with the Gain knob to dial in the exact right level of distortion, and Master Volume controls the final product—the loudness of the sound coming out of your amp.

The other types of controls that almost every amp has are tone controls. These are labeled High (also called Treble), Mid (not surprisingly, for the middle-range frequencies), and Bass, or Low. The best way to use these is to experiment freely and listen closely to the differences they create in your sound. Turn your Treble all the way up—your guitar will probably start sounding tinny or shrill. Turn your Bass all the way up; notice how it gets kind of muffled sounding. Using tone controls is like picking the exact shade of your favorite color when you paint your room: the differences between shades, or tones, are subtle, but important. Every room affects the tone differently, so it's good to listen critically to amp sounds that you like and learn how to use your tone knobs to reproduce those sounds. Most electric guitars also have tone knobs.

Some amps have different channels. These amps will have two different sections on the control plate, each with its own Tone and Volume controls, and a Master Volume that affects both channels, usually to the far right. You can set each channel to a different sound, and switch between them using a foot switch or the Channel switch button. This can be handy if you want to switch from distortion to clean in the middle of a song without using a distortion pedal. A Drive switch button allows you to dial in two different types of distortion and switch between them.

Some newer amps also have digital effects built into them. These amps can be programmed to produce a whole array of different guitar sounds and effects. Playing with these sounds can be fun, and is a good way to learn about the differences between the different amp and guitar sounds, but there's no substitute for the real thing. If you find a sound you like programmed into your amp, I suggest listening carefully to that sound and figuring out how to create it yourself.

Amp Tricks and Troubleshooting

All amps are a little bit different, but the following will give you the basics you need to start experimenting with your sounds.

There are four types of volume:
1. Volume, also known as Level, Post, or Main.
2. Gain, also known as Pre or Drive.
3. Instrument Volume, the control on your guitar/bass/keyboard.
4. Master Volume—Playing with all three of the above volumes will change your sound in various ways. Once you have found the tone you like, you can simply make it louder, without losing the cool thing you've got going, by turning up the Master Volume.

TRICKS

For more distortion:

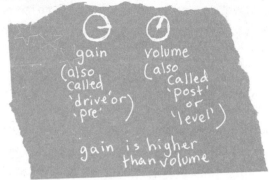

▶ Turn your Instrument Volume all the way, or almost all the way, up.

▶ Set your Master Volume to a comfortable level.

▶ Turn your Gain up until you get the distortion you like.

For less distortion:

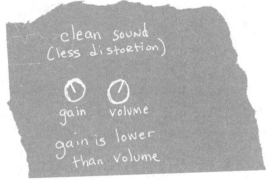

▶ Turn down the Gain.

▶ Turn down the Instrument Volume.

▶ Turn up the Master Volume.

For feedback:

▶ Follow the above directions for distortion, but turn your amp Gain even higher. (Remember, Gain can be called Drive or Pre depending on your amp.)

▶ Turn up the volume on your guitar.

▶ Face your amp and move in close to it with your guitar.

To stop feedback:

➡ If a guitar or bass is feeding back, just muffle the strings with your hand. It'll usually stop. You can also turn your Gain and/or Volume down to decrease feedback, or move farther away from your amp.

Some of these terms might be switched around on your particular amp. Don't be afraid to turn the controls up and down until you've found what you like. When you find sounds you like, it can be very helpful to either write down the numbers for each control, put a tiny strip of tape pointing to where you like the knob to be, or draw a picture of each control and where it is turned.

TROUBLESHOOTING

Everything is so loud—I can't hear myself!

Position your amp so that you can hear yourself and your bandmates. If you are standing right in front of your amp and your amp is on the ground, you probably won't be able to hear yourself very well. Try tilting your amp back so that it points more toward your head, setting it on a chair, or taking a couple of steps away from your amp.

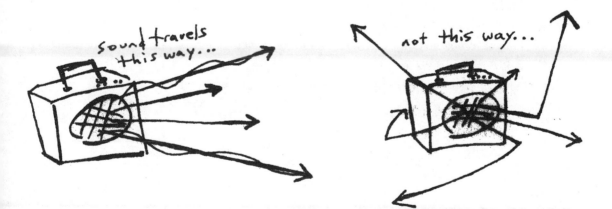

My amp won't turn on!

This is often an easy problem to solve. Chances are you've either blown a fuse or you need a new electrical cord. An amp fuse looks like a little black plug with white lettering on it. The fuse screws into your amp, usually somewhere on the back. Pull your fuse out, then put it back in—sometimes they jiggle loose and this will solve the problem. If your fuse is missing or you think it might be blown, go to a music store

and get another one—they're cheap. If you are playing a lot of shows, it is a good idea to have an extra fuse handy—that way you can just replace it on the spot and keep playing.

If your cord is blown, you'll need to take your amp in to a shop that has a repair person and get it replaced. Again, this won't cost much and shouldn't take very long.

My amp crackles and hisses!

If it's a tube amp, you might need new tubes. Tubes need to be replaced every few years to keep them sounding their best. If your amp is solid state, it's possible that some of the wiring has come loose. Take it to a repair shop. If your amp is humming or growling, it's possible that you've plugged into a circuit that has a neon sign, dimmer switch, or other interfering electrical appliance. If you can figure out what it is, turn it off; otherwise consider switching to a different outlet.

THREE WAYS TO BLOW UP YOUR AMP!

1. Turn every volume knob and every tone knob all the way up and play as hard as you can.
2. Get your amp wet.
3. Mismatch the electrical load between your amp and your speakers.

To avoid disaster, don't play with everything turned all the way up, keep your amp dry, ask a knowledgeable friend or a music store employee about the products you are using, and last but not least, take your amp to get serviced every few years.

TIPS FOR ROCK SINGERS

by Teri Untalan

Here are a few tips for singing into a microphone. Make sure to sing into the center of the microphone at all times. You should be about a finger-width away from it, except when singing in the extreme parts of your range. For soft, spoken parts, get right up on the microphone. For shouting or very loud singing or short bursts of volume, back off the microphone, but stay centered.

- If you start to get tired, then REST, REST, REST. Drink water. Do some deep breathing.
- Encourage your band to play at half volume during part of practice if you are getting fatigued. It's not a good idea to sing at full volume for several hours of band practice a day.
- Get good levels. Set the volumes on your mic and the instrument amps in the room so you can hear yourself and the instruments in a comfortable balance. Avoid getting into **volume wars** or straining your voice.
- Get good EQ. If your voice sounds too thin, brittle, or shrill, turn down the High (Treble) knob on the PA, or turn up the Low (Bass), or both. If your voice sounds boomy or muffled, turn up the Highs and turn down the Lows.
- Don't point your microphone at the speakers, as this will cause ugly, painful feedback. Don't unplug your microphone while the PA is on or it will POP! really loudly.
- Don't be shy about asking your guitarist or keyboardist to give you the starting note or chord. During rehearsal, if you have trouble finding melody lines, ask the guitarist to play some chords to help you find melodic ideas.
- When you're comfortable with the song, practice facing away from your bandmates. Set up as if you are onstage. Ask a couple of friends to come and be your band practice audience.

CHECK, CHECK!

IS THIS THING ¿ON?

BY BETH WARSHAW-DUNCAN

As you can see, plugging in takes practice, too. Learning the ins and outs of your gear during rehearsal will make your time onstage easier. It's important to be comfortable onstage and it's important to ask for what you need so that you can play the best show possible. Chances are, at some point you will need to work out the details of your sound with the person running the soundboard. Soundpeople speak a language of their own, and to communicate with them, you must learn some words in their native tongue. The following phrases will get you started on your journey toward being happy, comfortable, and able to hear yourself and your bandmates onstage.

I NEED AN XLR CABLE.

I need one of those heavy cords with different ends—one end has three little prongs in a triangle and the other end has three little holes in the same pattern—that plug into a microphone and a soundboard.

PASS ME THAT ¼-INCH CABLE.

Pass me that cord that has two matching ends—both metal plugs about 1 inch long—so I can plug my guitar, bass, or keyboard into my amp.

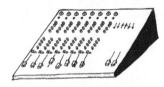

I'M PLUGGED IN THROUGH THE BOARD (OR SOUNDBOARD OR MIXING BOARD).

So it can be heard, my instrument is plugged in to the big piece of equipment that houses the mixing board, where a soundperson makes sure everyone is plugged in, and everyone is heard, by pushing volume knobs, or faders, up and down.

CAN I GET A DIRECT BOX (OR DIRECT INPUT BOX OR D.I. BOX)?

Can I get a small box that connects to the soundboard on one end and my instrument on the other? It's an alternative to playing through an amp.

HOW DOES IT SOUND IN THE MIX?

How does it sound when we're all plugged in and playing together? Is it loud enough? Is it too loud? Can you hear each instrument and the vocals clearly? Does it sound shrill, or tinny, or muffled?

I NEED MORE GUITAR IN THE MONITORS.

I'm sound-checking or playing a show, but I can't hear any guitar and I need the sound-person to make the guitar louder in the speakers on stage. I use those speakers to listen back to myself and the band's sound.

CAN YOU BOOST MY LEVELS?

Can you make my instrument or my voice in the monitors louder? I can't really hear it.

THE GUITAR IS BLEEDING INTO MY VOCALS.

The guitar sound is being picked up by a nearby mic meant for someone else. It makes the guitar sound louder because the sound is coming through two mics instead of one.

CAN YOU GET RID OF THE FEEDBACK?

Can the soundperson get rid of that screechy sound by lowering the levels?

OUR LOAD-IN IS AT 4:30 P.M. AND OUR SOUND CHECK IS AT 5 P.M.

We need to be at the club at around 4:30 P.M. to drop off our equipment and start setting it up. At around 5 P.M., we'll set everything up on stage and play a couple of songs so that the soundperson can get a good balance of sounds when the audience isn't around. If we're playing first, we can usually leave our gear in place; if there's another band playing first, we usually have to move our gear to the side of the stage.

to learn about sound equipment. I would also suggest getting in touch with people at local recording studios and seeing if you can intern or volunteer. Most music stores have a section with recording gear. Prices may vary from store to store, so shop around for a good price.

Once you secure access to equipment—start playing! You can record yourself, your friends, siblings, whomever. Practice and learn the ins and outs of your equipment. Be patient. Trust yourself. Learn to troubleshoot. Practice ingenuity.

CASSETTE TAPES/CASSETTE RECORDER

Go to your local drug store and buy a pack of cassette tapes. This will cost about $5.

You can purchase a portable cassette recorder at an electronics store or a store with an electronics department for about $20 to $30. It's also pretty easy to find a cassette recorder at a thrift store or a garage sale.

Cassette recorders are cheap and easy to use. To record with a cassette recorder, arrange your amps like you normally would during band practice. Make sure everybody can hear themselves and each other. Everybody's volumes should be more or less equal. Place the tape recorder someplace off the ground (like a chair or a table) in a corner of the room. Then press Record and play your song.

If you are using drums, try playing in a bigger room to eliminate distortion. If one instrument is too loud or too quiet, adjust the volume of the amps and vocal PA to get a mix you like. You can also move the tape recorder around the room to find the best place to get the mix you're after.

CASSETTE 4-TRACK

There was a time not that long ago—in the '60s–when 4-track cassette decks were the state of the art for everyone, including the Beatles. In the '90s, a lot of beautiful lo-fi, indie rock recordings were made on 4-tracks by musicians playing around in their bedrooms and basements. These days it might be easier to record and mix on a computer, but 4-tracks are still popular and are a really good hands-on way to learn the ins and outs of recording. Just like any other art form, the more tools you have in your toolbox, the better artist or musician or recording engineer you will be. Four-tracks are also way cheaper than computers.

Cassette 4-tracks can be found in music stores and typically cost between $100 and $400. You can also look for a used one on Craigslist.org or at a second-hand instrument store. (Try to get the operating manual if you buy a used 4-track.)

To record with a 4-track, you will need a microphone ($40–$100), a microphone cable ($15), and an instrument cable ($15). If you are serious about recording, it's worth the money to buy a decent microphone. It is also helpful to have headphones so that you, the engineer, can hear what you are recording as opposed to only being able to hear what the band sounds like live in the room.

With a cassette 4-track, you can layer different instruments and voices and record your band on four separate channels, each with its own volume and tone controls. This will give you more control than a cassette recorder over how the different instruments are mixed together in your final product. Decide whether you would like to do live recordings by recording multiple instruments playing at once, or if you'd rather record each instrument individually (track by track). Set up your connections, including headphones to listen to playback, according to the manual.

If you choose to do a live recording, you can either mic the room, or plug each instrument or mic into the 4-track. Miking the room can be as easy as putting a couple of mics on stands in the middle of the room. If you are using electric guitars and basses, it's probably better to mic your amps. Arrange your amps and adjust your volumes, press Record, and adjust the levels and the mic placement until you like the sound you are getting in your headphones. Listen for **bleed**, which is when the sound from one instrument is being picked up by the mic for a different instrument. Arrange your amps and instruments so that you have as little bleed as possible.

If you want to record one track at a time, pick one instrument to go first and be the track everybody plays along with when they record their parts. This track is called the **basic track**. Basic tracks are usually rhythmic—bass and drums, or rhythm guitar. You'll have to rig up headphones for the musicians to wear while they play so that they can hear the basic tracks.

DIGITAL 8+ TRACK RECORDING PROGRAM

Recording with a computer program is similar to recording with a cassette 4-track, but it's done digitally. This means that instead of your song being recorded on a cassette tape, it is recorded onto your computer's hard drive. The biggest noticeable difference between a digital recording and an analog recording is that while the analog sound is warmer, digital sound is clean, easy to copy, move, and loop, and easy to convert into MP3 files or burn onto a disc.

Some inexpensive digital-recording software programs include GarageBand (Mac), Cubase (Mac or PC), Cakewalk (PC), ACID (PC), and Sonar (PC).

To get started with digital recording, you will need an audio interface (audio card), a microphone, an XLR-to-¼-inch microphone cable ($15), a ¼-inch-to-⅛-inch (or miniplug) adapter, and a regular ¼-inch (instrument) cable. You can purchase the software and the equipment at most music stores.

Audio Interfaces—Most computers require you to plug your microphones and instruments into an audio interface, which then plugs into your computer's Audio In jack. Audio interfaces range in type from sound cards with a line in, mic, and stereo output to USB and Firewire multitracking consoles that have two, four, or eight or more inputs that can record simultaneously, or track by track. Talk to teachers, friends, or a customer-service representative at the music store to help you choose.

Plug-ins (effects)—Most basic audio recording programs come with audio plug-ins—digital effects that can manipulate the sounds recorded in your project. There are several different types of effects including delay, chorus, flange, gate, pitch shift, and distortion, as well as reverb, the most commonly used effect. Reverb can make your audio track sound like it was recorded in a large room, indoor swimming pool, gymnasium, bathroom, closet, hallway, or a tunnel. It can make the vocal or instrument track you're recording sound like it's close or far away, or in front of or behind you.

Some amps have effects built in, or you can use an effects pedal. If you record with effects, you can't remove them during the mix. If you record clean (with no effects), you can add effects after recording, during mixing.

Mixing and Mastering

After you've recorded all the sounds you will be working with, you can begin the process of blending the different recorded channels into one cohesive sound.

MIXING

Mixing is the process of setting the tones (equalizing, or EQing, the treble, bass, and midrange qualities of the sound), adjusting the volume levels, and panning each recorded track so that the vocals and instruments have a pleasing sound and each part can be heard. This process becomes more complex the more tracks you have.

EQing

EQing is the process of using the Treble, Mid, and Bass controls to achieve a sound that is balanced and natural and as close as possible to the actual sounds of the instruments and voices you have recorded

Setting Volumes

Setting the volumes involves making the quieter sounds in a recording loud enough to be heard and bringing down the volume of the louder sounds so that they don't overwhelm the mix.

Panning

Panning assigns sounds to the left, right, or center of the mix. When you listen to music through headphones, do you ever notice that different things are happening in each ear at the same time? When you listen to a band's CD, you cannot see the musicians, but the panning of the instruments gives you a mental picture of where the sounds are coming from.

The concept of stereo is based around four directions. Left and right are controlled by panning, in front and behind are controlled by effects. The combination of effects and panning can give each instrument its location in the mental picture produced by a listener. Panning can make a huge difference in making your recording sound good.

MASTERING

Mastering is the final step. Mastering is the process of raising and compressing the levels, and making sure that all of the songs on a CD are of comparable volume. Most mastering is done by professionals with specialized equipment, although mastering programs are also available.

Scene

How do you go from playing by yourself to playing in a band? What do you do if all the places where music happens in your town are "21 and over"? How do people find out about your band and your friends' bands?

One of the best things about playing music is that you can do it with and for other people. Music opens doors to lifelong friendships and inspiring collaborations. In this chapter we cover the basics of finding a place to play and people to play with, and how to start getting your music out into the world.

HOW i GOT OUT OF MY BeDROOM

(in eleven lessons)

BY MIRAH YOM TOV ZEITLYN

When I started teaching myself how to play the guitar and write songs, I was eighteen years old. Not incredibly young, not incredibly old. I didn't have a plan of what to do with the music I had begun to make. Now, fifteen years since my humble beginnings of strumming one chord furtively in my bedroom, I am the proud owner of one bona fide music career. It can be a perplexing navigation, trying to figure out how to turn something you love into something other people can love, and especially hard to figure out how to make a living from it. What I have to offer you here is a brief history of my "band" and a few lessons I learned along the way.

#1 In 1993, I was a student at Evergreen State College in Olympia, Washington. Though there was already a strong music scene in Olympia, I felt somewhat alienated from it. I remember going to a Bikini Kill show downtown, standing outside the Capitol Theater and looking through the open door at all the girls inside and then deciding to just walk home. It should have been a very inclusive situation. I was a girl, I believed in the power of like-minded people gathering together, I was starting to make music, too. But I went home instead of joining in. I didn't feel cool enough to stay.

Lesson: Everyone is cool enough. Period. If you find that you are comparing yourself to others, remember that it's okay to have moments of self-doubt. Just try to have at least twice as many moments of absolute certainty.

#2 The Olympia music scene was specifically supportive of young women musicians and artists getting out and being loud and heard, but I mostly just sat at home in my bedroom and wrote songs on my acoustic guitar. I didn't think my music fit in very well with the musical aesthetic popular among most of my peers. My songs were melodic and quiet. I didn't do much yelling or screaming.

Lesson: Not all music has to be loud. Loud isn't the only way to express yourself and be heard. You might just be a strong person who makes quiet music, like me. If loud is how you feel, be loud! If soft is how you feel, be soft! But always be authentically and proudly yourself.

#3 Although I'd always loved to sing, I was still quite a novice guitar player. This—what I perceived as my inadequacy—made me keep my music mostly to myself. Looking back now, I can see that my private sort of feeling had a purpose. I was teaching myself how to write songs and how to play my instrument, learning about what I liked and what I didn't. I was learning to communicate and make decisions with myself, the same way that people in bands spend time learning how to communicate with each other about how to make music that they all love.

I wanted to try recording some of my songs, so I set up a boom box and recorded myself onto a cassette tape and then played the tape back while recording a second track onto another boom box. The first track was just me singing and playing my guitar, and when I played it back and recorded again I added extra vocals and more guitar. It was very simple, very lo-fi.

Lesson: You can be a band even if you are only one person. If you have ideas for more sounds than you can make at one time, try recording yourself at home. No matter how un-fancy your equipment or techniques, you will be amazed at how fun it is to listen to yourself and then add tracks. You will learn a lot. A cassette 4-track or a computer will work, but I would even suggest the boom box technique for a first try. The stakes are pretty low and boom boxes are very user friendly and cheap!

#4 The first song I ever wrote was a homework assignment. Good thing the assignment wasn't to make a peanut butter and jelly sandwich. I can only imagine how differently my life would have turned out. I decided to take some classes to learn about the basics of multitrack recording, mixing consoles, microphones, and, most important, about not being afraid of wires and cables and dials.

Lesson: **If you start using technology you will learn how to use it.** You don't have to master the art of recording or doing live sound in order to be a working musician, but having a familiarity with the tools and terms really helps.

#5 I finally started playing a few shows out—an open mic here, a **house show** there. I had spent enough years just watching other people play in bands and sing their songs, and finally knew I just had to try it or I would never get over my hesitation. It was scary at first. I would get very nervous and I felt like I still didn't really know how to play the guitar. My fingers would grip the neck so tightly my whole hand would ache for hours afterward. But it got better each time. I had a lot of close friends who were also just starting to play music, and we would set up shows for ourselves, make beautiful posters, maybe some cookies. Sometimes it would be just us, playing music for each other and eating the cookies we had made, but it was still satisfying, and good experience. There we were, practicing our future craft in a safe supportive environment of our own design. Perfect.

Lesson: **When you start playing shows, try to make them as fun as possible.** Play for your friends, have a house show. If your goal is to get comfortable with performing, all experience is good experience. Find the other people in your town whose music you like and invite them to play shows with you.

#6 I had a volunteer shift at our local food co-op and one day while I was washing lettuce and singing to myself, one of the co-op staff members, who happened to also have a very small record label and recording studio, introduced himself to me. We made fast friends and he offered to record me at his studio, as he was impressed with how nicely I sang while washing the lettuce.

Lesson: **Find out about your recording options.** Talk to people you know who play music. Besides playing shows, recording and sharing or selling your recordings is one of the best ways for people to hear your music. There are lots and lots of home-recording studios out there, friends of friends who would be excited to record you for free or very little. People who take care to have a bunch of microphones and mixing consoles around love to use them. You don't need to release your very first recordings, though you can. Use recording as a means to learn about how to make the music you most want to hear.

#7 Some months later, I had my first record album completed, a one-sided 12-inch. I was as surprised by it as any new parent and wasn't quite sure of the next moves, how to care for the little thing. My very small record label friend set up a mini **tour** to promote the album. It was from Olympia to San Diego and back and it was not always very fun. I was initiated into the strange club of people who travel far from their home, play music for strangers, and then sleep on their floors afterward. It was at times amazing and at times awkward, as most things in life can be.

Lesson: **Not all shows will be fun.**

#8 I went back home and continued to try and carve something out of almost nothing, out of just an idea. The idea was that I was going to record my songs and put them on records and people would listen to them. Then I would travel through their towns and play them a music show. A very simple idea really, not particularly original, but time-honored and holding a certain degree of mystique, which was attractive to me. I'd sort of tried it already. I'd had the good fortune of being recorded in a studio and taken on a little tour, but I felt very separate from the experience. I realized that I needed to have more self-initiative, more of a personal vision, in order to dig in to my desires.

I recorded more songs, some on my now delightfully outdated cassette 4-track, some with a friend who happened to be a recording genius in the studio to which he had access. I was happy with my new recordings and wanted people to hear them, so I made a tape. A cassette tape! I hand-letter-pressed, hand-cut, and hand-folded the carton. I sewed a little book into each one with images and some credits. I sewed a little paper button and a string onto the outside flaps so it could be secured. It was lovely and I could look at it and feel myself represented there.

Lesson: **Make it yourself! Make it yourself! Make it yourself!** I can't stress this enough. You will have plenty of time to have other people help you make things later. In the beginning, and maybe forever, make it yourself.

#9 My first tour was followed by another, and then more, always set up in those early years by my traveling companions. Later, after I'd learned the ropes and

started making more personal connections with people who put on shows, I set up tours myself as well.

Lesson: Setting up tours is really a matter of building a network. If you are a solo act, all you need are a car, a map, an e-mail account, and a few months to plan. You can start within a very small radius and before you know it, you will have a great outward-reaching spiral of folks who make and/or love music and love to put on shows in their town. Make friends through music with people who are in bands and go on tour with them, even if just for a weekend. Try to play shows with bands that are slightly more well known than you.

#10 I continued recording, by myself and with my friends. My recordings tended to sound more like a band than like a "solo act," thanks to the endless possibilities of multitrack recording, and eventually, I decided to actually have a band to play with live. I'd gotten to know lots of musicians over the years, through friends and through touring and recording, and so I started asking folks to play in my band. It was sometimes hard to teach other people how to play my songs since I was self-taught and not very music theory–oriented, but with perseverance and a bit of mime we accomplished the task.

Lesson: You can change. You can start off in a loud rock band and then decide that you really like to sing cabaret. Or you can start off as a solo singer/songwriter and then decide you want to play with a full orchestra and a heavy metal drummer. You can do anything you want.

#11 I kept recording and touring, and within a few years I had quite a little stack of albums bearing my name. This is the period when I really started feeling established in my identity as a musician. I'd already gone through the initial emergence, the awkward adolescence, and then finally, a sort of blossoming, an acceptance of who I was and what I wanted. It took many years!

Lesson: Grow, trust yourself, and work hard. Never stop actualizing your ideas. Just because you may have started out plunking around on a guitar alone in your bedroom doesn't mean you won't end up making album after album, having a band, and touring the world. If you like the music you make, then other people will like it, too.

GETTING READY TO PLAY ON STAGE

by Marisa Anderson

Here are a few tips to help you and your band feel ready to play your songs in front of an audience!

Run through the songs as if you are at the venue.
Turn your practice room into an imaginary stage and put yourself on it. Pick up your instruments and plug them in. Run through the songs. Remember to face the (imaginary) audience while making sure everybody in your band can see each other as much as possible.

It's okay to be nervous.
Talk about it! Even the most experienced performers get scared or anxious before a show. Don't forget to breathe. You are the only one who knows your songs inside and out, so if you mess up a little bit no one will notice, especially if you just keep on playing and don't react.

Stay focused and have fun!
As long as your band is focused on the music and listening to each other, nothing can go too wrong. In fact, time will probably fly out the window and your **set** will be over before you know it because you are having so much fun!

Before you get on stage, ask yourself:
- Do I have my pick? Do I have my drumsticks?
- Do I know the lyrics/do I have my lyric sheet?
- Is my guitar/bass tuned?
- Do I know where to stand?
- Do I know where to plug in?
- Do I have my pedals?
- Do I know how my song starts?
- Are my shoes tied?
- Is my zipper up?
- Are all of my bandmates feeling good and ready to go?

119

STARTiNG A BAnD

BY CAREY FAY-HOROWITZ

I have started many bands over the years, and found that there is no particular key to ensuring their success. My bands have started in a variety of settings and situations, and often the ones that seemed most doomed at the beginning have turned out to be the most fun and successful.

When starting a band, there are several objectives, but these can be pursued in any order:

▶▶ You will want to learn how to play an instrument (and/or use your voice).

▶▶ You will need to come up with bandmates and a name for your band.

▶▶ You will need a practice space and equipment on which to play your instruments, like amps and a PA.

But none of these things are necessarily required. I have been in bands with people who didn't know how to play their instruments at all, and had no intention of learning. There have been times when none of us owned any instruments or had a practice space. I have had countless nameless bands, some of which even played shows before we named ourselves. However, I recommend trying to cover most of these basic needs if you are serious about starting a band that will be fun to play and explore with, and that may last for a while.

The first band I started was in ninth grade, with three other girls. We had a name, which I now forget—something with "sparkle" in it—but we never actually played music together. I was the only one who took more than one lesson. Still, it was a significant band for me because it got me to start playing drums, and twelve years later I'm still playing.

I spent the rest of high school playing drums mostly alone. My excuse was that I needed to practice more before I started playing in a real band, but really I was just too shy to ask anyone to play music with me. What I didn't realize then was that there was only so much I could learn by myself; I would improve exponentially just by playing with other people.

I brought my drum set to college and kept it stacked in the dorm room closet. Eventually, some friends and I started a band. The four of us each had names starting with one of the first four letters of the alphabet, so I came up with the name The Alphabetical Order. But soon our D in the Alphabetical Order went to Ethiopia for a year abroad, and the B graduated, and we weren't much of an alphabet anymore.

Up to this point, I didn't really consider myself a drummer. Drumming was just one of my hobbies. After college, I started playing more on my own, and became more determined to start a band. I started dating a guitarist and liked his songs a lot, so we began playing music together. We found a friend to play bass, and we liked playing together so much that even after the guitarist and I stopped dating, the band stayed together. For the first time, I was starting to play shows, real shows at real venues—but our band didn't have a name! I think we might have even called ourselves Nameless for a while. We played three shows before finally settling on the Moods for a name.

The Moods recorded some songs in a friend's studio, which is the first recording I had of any of my bands. That's another important lesson I later learned: record your songs. I would love to hear some of the songs I wrote with other bands, but at the time we thought we'd remember those songs forever, and that we'd continue to play as a band for the rest of our lives. And of course now I have no recollection of what most of those songs sounded like.

After the Moods ended, I tried out playing with a few different bands that I found on Craigslist. In some ways, finding bands this way can be ideal. Everyone gets a chance to discuss their influences, interests, and goals before even meeting, so once the band forms people have all communicated about what kind of commitment they are making. But it can also be intimidating to play music with total strangers.

After six years of living in New York, it was time for a change, so I moved out West and made it one of my top goals to start a band. The other goals were to plant a garden and get a cat. I achieved all three goals, surprising even myself with how fast things came together. Sometimes all you need is to find the right community, and everything will fall into place.

The first band I started out here was called the Cars the Doors, a bicycle-themed band that experienced a type of success that was unprecedented for me, and shocking as well, considering that our bass player refused to learn how to properly play the bass. At shows he would often throw his bass on the floor—I do not recommend this!—and then throw himself on the floor as well, going into some sort of controlled seizure, while the guitarist and I would attempt to hold the song together. Even though he couldn't play the bass and liked to break things on stage, our bass player's energy and creativity went a long way, and we quickly became a performance-based band, one that people would watch more for the visual entertainment than for the music. Somehow, without trying very hard, we got written up in weekly papers and popular fanzines, and even made some money touring the country. The Cars the Doors was an example of how little you actually need to start a band. We formed having no equipment of our own, and only two-thirds of our band knew how to play our instruments. We had no practice space and very little money. But up to this point, that band was my most successful musical project.

Eventually the Cars the Doors split up, and the guitarist and I got a new bass player and formed a new band with the goal of going on tour in Europe with some friends who were in a band in France. We moved quickly, writing songs and recording a CD in a friend's living room, all within a few months of forming the band. We played a handful of shows at local venues, and then we headed to France for a two-week tour.

Now that people knew I was a pretty good drummer, I starting getting invited to play in other bands. A band called Songs for Moms, whom I met through a mutual friend, asked me to play with them, and I instantly fell in love with their music. I was determined to play in their band, so I listened to their songs every day and tried to learn the drumbeats. When we finally practiced together, we clicked instantly. This

time, playing music with total strangers worked out really well. Almost two years later, they are two of my best friends and we are about to put out our second album.

Looking back on all these stories and bands, it seems that one key to success has been to set goals for the band, like going on tour, or recording an album. Without goals, the band risks becoming stagnant, and everyone's motivation will quickly dissipate. The bands that have been most positive for me have been the ones where we set goals, like going on tour or recording an album, before our enthusiasm begins to wane.

As long as having fun is always the number one-goal, the rest is easy. Just pick up an instrument you like to play, grab some friends, and rock!

BAND FORMATION!
by Elizabeth Venable

Here are a few tips on finding people for your band:

➡ Ask your friends. If they don't know how to play an instrument maybe they want to learn.

➡ Go see live music. Could you imagine any of those musicians playing in your band? Ask them if they're interested in having a second project. Also, the more you go see live bands the more likely you are to run into people who like the same music as you. Introduce yourself; maybe they're looking for people to play with, too.

➡ Place an ad in the paper or online stating what you're looking for and the kind of music you're interested in playing.

Booking youR First ShOW

BY BECKY GEBHARDT

You've been writing and rehearsing, and now you're ready to perform live on stage! The time has come to share your art with the world!

Find the Venue that Fits YOU

Your first step in booking your first show is to find a venue that fits you. When choosing a venue, ask yourself:

▶▶ How many people do I realistically think will show up at my **gig**?

▶▶ Where do my friends and I go to see local music?

▶▶ Does my style of music seem compatible with the type of acts that normally play at the venue where I want to play?

▶▶ Is the venue all ages? Do I need it to be?

A coffee shop or small club is a great place to play a first gig. Other types of shows to consider are community events, house concerts, or parties. Ask a fellow musician if you can open for them. Building a community with other local artists is not just an excellent business strategy, it is what makes the effort worthwhile and fulfilling at the end of the day. Music should not be about competition, but about supporting each other and being a witness to each other's growth and accomplishments.

CONTACTING THE VENUE

Come up with a list of a few places you'd like to play, and find a couple of dates that work for you. Ideally, booking a gig at least a month, if not three months (or more!), in advance is best. Find out the name of the person who books music at that venue. You can go to the venue in person, call the venue, look online, or look in local newspapers. Don't be discouraged if it's not easy to get in touch with a booker; just stay friendly and persistent.

When you talk to the booker, tell them a little bit about who you are and what you do. Ask what their booking policies and requirements are. Questions to ask include:

▶▶ Is there a **guarantee**, or does the band get paid out of the **door**? (See pages 130 and 138 for more on these terms and financial arrangements.)

▶▶ Is the band responsible for paying the **door person** and the soundperson?

▶▶ Can the band supply its own door and soundperson?

▶▶ What is the sound system like? Are there any restrictions/requirements as far as sound?

▶▶ How many bands does the venue book on one **bill**? How long does each band play?

The most organized booker will have everything you need to know posted on the venue's website or be able to e-mail the information to you.

If you feel like you can meet the requirements, then talk dates and see if they're willing to book you on the date you want. You might be asked to provide a demo CD (see page 133), press kit (see page 132), or a link to a website featuring your band's information, photos, and music (see page 152).

Once you have booked a show, be very clear on the following info:

▶▶ What time is **load-in** and **sound check**?

▶▶ What time does the show start?

▶▶ What time does our band play? Where are we in the order of bands?

▶▶ How do you settle the door money?

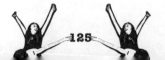

Some venues might require that you sign a contract. Be sure to read it, consider asking someone else to read it, and discuss any questions you have with the booker.

FOLLOW-UP

Remember, if you have a good experience with a gig, it's important to nurture the contact. Call or e-mail the booker the next day to say thank you. If you're ready to book another show, the sooner you do it the better.

Publicity

The show is booked—now what? It's time to spread the word!

INTERNET

Online marketing is important, easy, and free! Start by sending an e-mail to your friends with all the show information. Include a map or directions to the venue, and any useful information like time, date, address, cover charge, age restrictions, if they serve an amazing latte, etc. Ask your close friends and family members (whomever you feel comfortable with) to forward your e-mail to their friends, along with a personal vote of confidence from them. If you've made a digital or print flier, attach it to your e-mail so people have a visual reminder and can print it out to give to friends.

Your friends and family are the beginning of your mailing list, which is how you will keep in touch with your ever-growing fan base.

Tap into existing online communities like MySpace, Facebook, etc., to create a profile for your musical act (see How to Spin the Web, page 152). Add friends and fans. Post your shows on your calendar, send out bulletins, and search for blogs and music-related websites where you can publicize your show.

Network with other artists and musicians who live near you. Musicians are usually more than willing to support each other (as they should be!). The limits to what can be done to promote your music via the Internet are infinite. Creativity and authenticity are important!

Many print publications also have an online version. Look up local newspapers, from mainstream to alternative weeklies to neighborhood rags. Calendar listings are always free, and guidelines to submit your event can be found on the publication's website, or you can always call and ask.

PRINT

Fliers, posters, and word of mouth are rock 'n' roll marketing mainstays. When you create a flier, especially your first one, you will be creating a relic, capturing a precious fledgling moment that you will treasure in years to come. Do it! Make four fliers on one 8½-by-11-inch piece of paper. You can hand-write or draw, use your computer, or both. Graphics and photos can make a flier more interesting and eye-catching. Be sure to include all the vital show information, and your web address if you have a website.

Give small handfuls of fliers to friends to give to their friends, post one on the bulletin board at work or school, etc. Take posters and fliers to coffee shops, record stores, rehearsal spaces, radio stations, the venue you're playing, and anywhere live shows are promoted! Maintain the courtesy of not covering up any other fliers, unless they're out of date. You might need to use pushpins, tape, or sometimes even staples, so be prepared with them all (or at least pins and tape).

Always ask the booker, promoter, or someone from the venue where you are playing if they have a list of media contacts that you can get in touch with about getting press for your show. Many venues will provide this because they are as interested in getting people to your show as you are. This can help focus your search for whom to contact from which media outlet. You can always reach out beyond the list, but it's a great place to start.

Calendar listings in print news publications are another great way to get your name out there! Go to your local library, music store, newsstand, and coffee shop to pick up all the local and regional newspapers and magazines (usually they're free except for major newspapers). Follow their directions on how to submit calendar events. Keep in mind that publication schedules vary and you might need to submit info several weeks in advance. The more advance notice you give, the more publicity you get, and that many more people will have the chance to see your event listing.

Another smart publicity move is writing and sending out a press release. Even if you don't distribute full press kits (see page 132), a simple press release can yield some effective publicity. A press release is a short description of your event (in this case, live music) and who you are, which you can send to any news publication (print or online). This brings your event to the attention of news staff with more information than a calendar listing alone can provide, and opens up the opportunity for an article or even small blurb to be written about your show. Every publication will provide information on how to submit a press release; it can vary a lot, so be sure to follow directions. You can always call and ask if you're not sure. This actually could be the best way to do it because then you have the chance to establish a personal connection.

You can search the Internet for examples of press releases so that you can see what they generally look like. There is a standard format, so try to see an example before you send. You want to stick to one page (two are rarely needed), try to find an interesting angle, be concise, and keep all vital details at the top. Imagine you are writing a mini-article about your show.

When you write a press release:

➡ List your contact information in the upper left-hand corner of the page.

➡ Write a headline, which is a statement that summarizes the point of your news.

➡ Write a series of paragraphs explaining your event and who you are. Information should be written from top to bottom in order of most to least important.

Writers may not have time or space to include everything you want to share, so they need to know what is vital. The first paragraph should be one or two sentences long, a to-the-point info byte answering who, what, where, and when. The following paragraph can delve into a little more detail: what does your music sound like, where are you from, do you have any notable accolades to share, who else is playing?

It's up to you to decide what's important to share. If you can create an interesting or unique angle, you will have more luck getting press. For example, maybe your show is a benefit, with proceeds being donated to a homeless shelter. That makes you stand out and adds worth to publicizing your event! If you send the press release digitally, you can also attach a photo if you have one.

Although it might seem intimidating, don't be afraid to look up the contact information for music or arts and entertainment writers and editors, and write to

them or call them to invite them to your show and ask them to preview it in their publication. Persistence is really important. They will tell you when, how, and where to send your digital or printed press release. Follow up with people to make sure

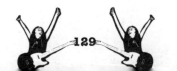

exibit 2: press release

NUN FACTORY
nunfactory@musictown.com
(xxx)xxx-xxxx
Playin' @ the BAT CAVE 1999 Cave Way
ROBIN ASKED US TO PLAY A
BENEFIT SHOW 2 REPAIR THE
BATMOBILE ~ WE SAID YES! COME
CHECK OUT NUN FACTORY
PLAYIN' LIVE W/ 2 COOL 2 ROCK,
THE CIRCLE A1 ~ PUNX NOT DEAD.
SUPPORT A GREAT CAUSE!
$5 SUGGESTED DONATION. FREE COOKIES!
$4 W/ COSTUME. 12-12-08, 7 PM
@ THE BAT CAVE!

they received your press release, and follow up again to see if they're going to print anything, and follow up again to invite them to the show. Don't nag, just be nice and your persistence will pay off. It's their job and yours!

RADIO

Which radio stations in your area are compatible with the type of music you make? Which radio stations support local music? Some Internet radio stations support independent artists—send them your music! Find out about these local and indie-friendly radio stations by talking to people who work at music stores, searching the Internet, and asking your friends.

Schools are the first place to look. Many colleges, universities, and sometimes even high schools host radio stations. These radio stations usually love to support local artists.

College and Internet radio is where serious music fans turn to hear new music. You are new, exciting music! They might be willing to play your demo CD on the air, promote your show, or have you come into the studio to do a live interview and performance. Call, e-mail, or walk in to the station to find out how to get the ball rolling.

WORD OF MOUTH

Definitely ask all your friends how they find out about new bands, where they hear new music, and where they see posters for shows. You might be missing a great publicity opportunity that you don't know exists, or is so obvious you don't even think of it.

Every show is a unique experience. Get people on board to support you as you venture into the realm of live performance. Share your music with the world, and start familiarizing people with your name. Even if they don't come to the show, people will start seeing your name on fliers and in calendar listings. Eventually they will remember who you are. The wise will come to your first shows so that they can say "I saw her when. . . ."

Money Matters

There are a few different ways that artists can get paid for playing shows. Sometimes the venue or promoter offers a **flat fee** to the artist for their performance. If there's a cover charge, you will split the collected money with the venue. Some shows are free for the audience, and sometimes the audience is asked to make a donation, which falls somewhere between a tip and a strict cover charge.

When you play a free show, the person who booked the show will most likely pass around a hat, box, jar, or any container to collect donations from the audience. If the audience has to buy tickets or pay a cover charge, a percentage of the total income from the door or the tickets will go to you, and a percentage will go to the venue. It is possible that other people (soundperson, door person, etc.) might need to be paid as well from that money. Be clear on money issues so that you don't have to deal with any problems on the day of the show. Collect your share of the door after your show, and understand how many people paid and what percentage was given to you.

What to Bring to the Show

GEAR

Sometimes venues have in-house gear such as a drum kit or a bass rig available to every band that plays there. Are you a soloist or band? What gear do you need and is there anything you won't need to bring because the venue will provide it? Finding out what gear the venue will provide can save you lots of time and effort hauling heavy equipment.

MERCH

Typical merchandise items include recordings of your music, stickers, buttons, and T-shirts. It's fun to be creative with this. You can talk to screen printers to get prices and possibly ideas for less common merch items like headbands, pencils, or mousepads.

Merchandise is an opportunity for you to spread your music, get your name out into the world, and make some extra money.

MAILING LIST

Pass around an e-mail list so people can sign up to find out about the next show or any other important news you have to share!

HOW TO Make a PRESS KIT

BY CONNIE WOHN

A press kit is an important visual, audio, and physical representation of your band and your music. A press kit can be a tool to open doors with bookers, agents, promoters, labels, and any other music industry types. Nowadays, with MySpace and Sonicbids promoting personality all over the Internet, it may seem like creating a press kit is unnecessary work, but a lot of industry people still appreciate the effort. Take the time to create one for yourself or your band. Create an online version as well as a paper version.

What does your unique and beautiful press kit do for you?

➡ Booking shows—Send it to promoters or venue owners to get shows so you can play live and build an audience; this is how tours are built.

➡ Getting more press—Send it to local and national press for album reviews, calendar listings, or articles.

➡ Record deals—Send it to record labels to solicit interest in your record. This is considered "shopping the record" with the goal of landing a record deal.

➡ Building a team—Send it out to booking agents and management to try and enlist a crew of great people to help you work on building your career.

Your press kit is an expression of you, your originality, and your music. Use your creativity to make it eye catching and unique from any other band's press kit.

Here are the elements found in most press kits—but don't stress if you don't have all of these things:

Photo. Take a fun black-and-white photo of you or your band. Choose a location that is special to you. Again, be original—this is all about you expressing yourself in a photo. If you are posting photos online for the purpose of reproducing in newspapers or magazines, make sure that they are at least 300 dpi.

Biography. Write a good one-page bio. Spend time describing yourself, your musical influences, cool bands you've played with, and any other noteworthy items. This is a colorful description of you on paper. Make it as special as you are! Make sure you include important details like contact information, the names and instruments of all the people in the band and anything that will distinguish you from the crowd.

Press. Add any press clippings you may already have. It is important for people to see who has written about you and what has been written. If you don't have any press yet, don't despair—that is what your press kit is being built to do . . . get you some press!

Music demo. Record a studio demo or a live show. Two or three songs are enough. The demo doesn't have to be studio quality; even a live recording is cool. And don't forget to put all-important contact info on that CD, to make it easier for those bookers and writers who get a ton of press kits and CDs every day.

Finally, combine all of these elements to make your press kit presentable to the recipients. Include your photo, bio, press clippings, and a copy of your most recent recording or demo. The press, record labels, promoters, booking agents, management companies, and any other people you may send it to will be happy to receive your press kit if it is organized and professional. Most of these people receive a dozen of these a day, so make sure yours stands out!

Sending out your press kit can be a lot of mailing, but that's how you get the word out about your band. It is crucial to follow up with a phone call about a week after you send your packet to make sure it has been received and that it isn't sitting in a pile of unopened mail. Calling will also help make a human connection to the press kit rather than it being just a slick bundle of papers and photos. Call, but don't nag!

Your press kit is a tool for opening doors to the greater music industry and to an audience who might like your music but doesn't live in your city or might not be able to come to your shows.

how to
MAKe AN ALL-AGES sHOW hAPPeN iN YOUR *TOWN*

BY STS

Anyone can organize and pull off a rad **all-ages** rock show. You don't need to have a promotional company, own a space with a stage, or even own any equipment. This is about finding the resources that are available in every town, be it a big city or a community of a thousand people, and using those resources to create your very own show. All-ages shows can draw toddlers, fourth graders, parents, your friends, and new people you've never met from neighboring towns. They are always meant to be a fun way for people to get together and enjoy music from your community and beyond.

There are just a few basic things you need to do to get started. Once you've decided you want to try your hand at organizing a show, you will need to:

➡ Find an all-ages venue or space.

➡ Find and confirm two or more bands/acts/performers to play the show.

➡ Make a flier, **handbill**, and/or poster and promote who's playing, when, where, and how much it costs.

➡ Acquire a PA system for the night and a person to run it.

➡ Attend and enjoy your own awesome show with your friends!

Finding the Space

First on the list is finding a place to have your show. This can be as easy as contacting a local all-ages venue already known for having shows and asking them for a date that is available. This should be done at least two months in advance if you already have a bill in mind, but sometimes venues will need up to six months to get you a good date and give you enough time to book your bill. Give yourself a lot of time if you're going to procure a venue first and then book the bands.

Be aware that club bookers often have lots of people calling them every day to set up shows; if you have to leave a message, remember to leave your name, phone number, and the dates you are interested in booking. Try to have at least a couple of dates that work so that, when you do get into a live conversation with a booker, if one date is already booked you can quickly suggest other possibilities.

If there's already a space in town that has all-ages shows and you want to go with them, just give them a call or e-mail and work out a date they can agree to hold for you. Even if they already have someone who does booking, most all-ages-friendly venues will be into you organizing your own show at their space. If there isn't such a space near you, or you want to try something new and exciting, it's time to start looking for, or creating, an alternative place to have a show.

Every town, no matter what the size, has at least a few spaces that can be very cool sites for all-ages shows. Here is the most important criterion you're looking for: a friendly venue manager or owner who is down with the youth scene and supportive of having a few bands playing in their space. Remarkably, venues operated by cool and encouraging people can be almost anywhere! Check out the following potential venues:

Bookstore/record store—Shopping while rocking! Ask the manager if they ever have in-store shows; many storeowners welcome the chance to create a buzz and sell some extra stuff.

Bowling alleys—Three words: Rock 'n' Bowl!

Café—Push aside those tables and chairs, get that acoustic performer on your bill, and punk (or chill) out!

Churches and synagogues—Many religious organizations will gladly offer you their basement without demanding performers or the audience be affiliated with them.

Diner/pizza parlor/burrito joint—If you're acquainted with the manager of a cool local dive, ask him or her about having a show. Didn't Hedwig play an all-ages buffet?

Garage/living room/barn—Totally DIY, but ask your mom first!

Grange halls—Old-fashioned and wonderfully useful sites built especially for the various needs of community members, including you.

Gymnasium—The acoustics might remind you of pep rallies and basketball practice, but totally cool venue anyway!

School—From preschools to colleges, all schools have large spaces that might be available for your event.

Swimming pool—An empty one, preferably, or set up on the edge and let people swim while you play! Your contact can be found through a community center or high school.

Teen/youth center—This is exactly what they're there for, and so are most likely a shoo-in for your show.

Theater—Keep in mind you'll probably have to work around their screening schedule. You might get to have a stage set for Hamlet as your background! Sometimes movie theaters will accommodate a cool event such as your show.

Other venues can include anywhere youths gather for fun: roller rinks, queer youth centers, the mall, skate parks and skate shops, and donut shops. Check out local ballrooms, dance halls, art spaces, warehouses, bike shops, farmers' markets, parks, amphitheaters, river boats . . . anywhere! I know of one all-ages show that happened in a beauty parlor, and a couple that happened in a *post office*—the lobby and the basement!

MAKING THE CONNECTION

Getting in touch with a venue owner or manager can be tricky, but there are several ways to try to track down the person in charge of the space you want to use.

➡ Use the Internet to search out a phone number or e-mail of someone who knows who's in charge of the space you're considering for your show.

➡ You can also use the phone book. Look under "Community" and see if a recreation center or grange hall comes up. It can be a little intimidating to call someone you don't know, and you may get a couple negatives in your search. But when that "Yes!" comes it could be the beginning of a great all-ages event booking relationship.

➡ If you know kids in bands, ask them where they play shows. Attend any all-ages shows in your area and take notes on which bands are playing and which venues support all-ages shows. Ask the adults you know if they can think of anywhere that might be down with an all-ages show.

➼ Networking sites such as MySpace can help you not only find a local venue, but also local and touring bands for your bill.

➼ A secret tip to finding where people are already creating a scene is to go to your local record and/or music instrument store and check out fliers already posted in their windows or on the counters. You can also strike up a conversation with someone behind the counter to find out if they know where any cool all-ages events are happening in town. If they don't know, it's definitely time to start booking your own!

Setting the Date and Time

Once you have someone interested in supporting your show with a venue, you need to agree on a good date and time. Friday and Saturday nights are awesome because most people don't have work or school the next day. Find out what the curfew is for kids under eighteen in your town and try to book the show so it ends by that time. A lot of all-ages shows try to accommodate a 10 P.M. curfew by starting the show at 7 P.M. so that it ends early enough to get home by 10 P.M. You'll also want to exert some control over the length of each set, and consider that if you have three bands that want to play forty-five minutes, they will need some time before and after their sets to set up and take down equipment.

Try to get the venue owner or manager to pencil you in on a couple options for dates. Once you get confirmation from bands that they can do the date, double-check that you aren't accidentally booking a show on a major holiday and contact the venue again to confirm the date. If at all possible, get this confirmation in writing!

The (Hidden) Costs of Rock Shows

Here's an overview of costs to consider when taking on a show.

VENUE RENTAL

When you book a venue, they may ask you for some money to rent the space. Be realistic. You can probably come up with a $100 rental fee from the door, but if the show is going to be small (10–100 people), $500 is way too much. Try to work out a mutually beneficial relationship that keeps your cost down. Sometimes local businesses will help offset costs if you put their name on the tiniest bottom corner of the flier. Always look for a place that's free (your house), or cheap (a community-oriented establishment), or one where at least you know you can cover the cost if no

one comes to the show. If it's a benefit show, that is, a fundraiser for a good cause, the venue may consider donating the space. Most venues will agree to a door split.

PA RENTAL

A PA is the only piece of equipment you are required to procure, unless you are lucky and the venue already has one. It doesn't have to be fancy, and many venues such as grange halls, churches, and cafes already have one. Small versions of these are called a vocal PA or practice PA. In a pinch, for quieter acts such as solo performers or duets, you can even plug a mic into a guitar amp to amplify the singer. This is not a great solution, but sometimes you gotta do what you gotta do!

In any case, it can't be said enough—you are in charge of making sure a PA is available at your show, so everyone can hear the preformance. (If you are unfamiliar with what a PA system looks like, do some quick research online or at a local music instrument store, or ask a friend who is in a band that uses a PA. Also see pages 88–92 in this book.) Bands will bring their own music equipment, but do not automatically bring their own PA to a show. As with all aspects of booking a show, try to procure one for free or cheap. Ask one of the bands if they don't mind letting you borrow theirs for the night. Ask a music store to donate a PA. Check with your venue to see if they have one tucked away in back for you to use. If it does cost money to rent the PA, don't spend so much that when you reimburse yourself there's no money left to pay the bands.

PAYING THE BANDS

Some bands expect to get paid, and some will play for free just for the fun of it or for a good cause. Always try to pay bands fairly. In order to avoid seeming a little slimy, do not offer a band publicity instead of payment. This tactic is seldom based in good motives. All bands deserve to get paid for their time and energy. Whether or not you can afford to pay them is another story. You can offer a percentage of your share of the door, or just ask them point blank if they wouldn't mind playing for free (dinner included?). For instance, if you have a 50/50 door split with the venue, you can take 50 percent of the door money and, after covering your costs, spread it evenly to all the bands on your bill.

Dealing with money can be frustrating, and sometimes gets personal or even political. The only way to handle money responsibly is to communicate and to be 100 percent honest about how much you think you can pay. Don't be secretive

about money—it just makes you look suspicious. If it's your first time booking a show, be honest about that, too.

It is good etiquette to find out if everyone on the bill is cool with paying the touring band more than the local bands. If your headliner has a huge draw, it is common to pay them more than the opening bands. Adopt a policy of being open and honest about money. Always check with the bands that they agree to the amount of money they may or may not get paid. If a band can't deal with what you're offering, you don't need to pretend you can get them more money. You might just wait to book them for a different show where you can guarantee them what they need. This is also your opportunity to be *very cool,* pay the bands fairly, and not take booking all-ages shows as an opportunity to make money for yourself.

PAYING THE SOUNDPERSON

Many venues charge to use a soundperson who can operate the PA. Try to get a soundperson who is into doing the show for free or cheap. Your best bet is to either learn how to use a PA and run sound yourself, or ask a savvy friend to help out. Many bands can run their own sound from a vocal PA and thus avoid paying a soundperson altogether. Just be sure you have a PA system and someone who knows how to set it up! It isn't very hard to do—it's one of those tech things that's actually easier than setting up a stereo.

ADVERTISING

You don't have to take out a newspaper ad to tell everyone about your show, but you will need to create and photocopy fliers, handbills, and posters to paper the streets. You definitely need to promote your show with 50 to 200 fliers, but some fancy-pants photocopy centers charge 8 cents a copy! Enter the photocopy hookup. This Grand Supporter of your cause will run some copies of your flier at his or her office, school, or other place of employment at minimal cost to you. It helps to bring your own paper and have the flier designed and ready to go, be it on a disk or a glue-stick-sodden napkin.

Fliers are the people's art! There are volumes of catalogs featuring posters of events through the ages. Make every flier beautiful and easy to understand, and keep at least one copy for posterity. Make sure your flier is legible and includes the names of the bands, the date, time, location, and cost, and to whom the money is going if it's a benefit show.

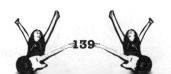

You might also wish to begin collecting names and addresses for a mailing list so you can send postcard invites for future shows. You can similarly send an e-blast with the show information, or post it on your blog. Whatever your advertising means turn out to be, save all your receipts and reimburse yourself for your costs from the door after the show.

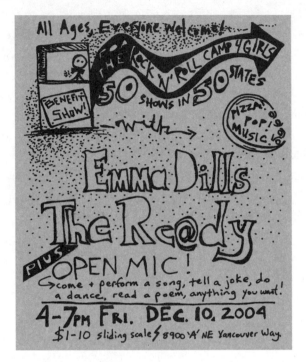

So, you've booked your best friend's toolshed, the local pancake house, or the place you took ballet lessons when you were five. If you haven't already started getting the bill lined up, now is the time. Finding bands to play can be as easy as booking your band, your best friend to read her new short story, those guys at your school, or doing something completely new to you.

Lining Up the Bill

Ask your friends, do a search on a friendly Internet networking site, or research small record labels to find out when your favorite performers are touring in your area. Many indie bands are totally open to show organizers e-mailing and inviting them to play all-ages shows. Don't limit yourself to only goth-metal cover bands or strictly punk shows if you can help it. Mix up your bills with all kinds of genres, ages, genders, abilities, and styles! Some of the best shows have had bills that consist of an opening puppet

show followed by some high-speed skate punk band and rounded out with an acoustic hip-hop crew from Albuquerque.

The Internet is your friend in this venture. If you are only familiar with big and fancy bands on the radio, this is a great time to discover the brilliance of small, independent bands and record labels. Almost all indie bands have a contact e-mail on their CDs. Do some research online, check out your local record store, and get yourself acquainted with bands that totally rule but don't get radio play. Most of these bands tour often, and many will take you up on your offer to book them a show, especially if you're organized and serious about setting up and promoting the show.

Getting Everyone on the Same Page

When it comes time to confirm with everyone, it's very important to be up on your game and ready to communicate exactly what everyone can expect. This is when you confirm with the venue the date, time, venue cost, and sound/PA needs. Tell the bands the order they will be playing and how much you think you can pay them, if at all, or at least what percentage of the door they can expect. Tell them if there's a touring band and if that will affect how much they get paid. Ask them if they want someone on the guest list. Tell them what time they should be at the venue to do a sound check.

A great way to completely finalize and confirm the event is to create a flier and give copies to the venue owner and bands. They can help promote the event, and take this as their last chance to back out.

Wait a Minute! What's in It for Me?

For some people, putting on a show is a form of artistic expression. For others, it's a way to throw a party with a purpose. Booking DIY all-ages shows is always an act of love. There is seldom money in it for the organizer. In fact, it is considered a sort of faux pas to take money or try to make a living as a DIY all-ages show organizer. This is a slightly odd tradition considering all the work you put into doing the event, but it boils down to one fact: You love music and you feel that all-ages shows are a great way for everyone to enjoy it. Many all-ages show organizers book hundreds of shows without ever considering taking money above covering their costs.

There are, however, a couple of ways commonly used to graciously defray your costs and ask for support of your music-happening efforts from the larger community:

NO ONE TURNED AWAY FOR LACK OF FUNDS

This is an alternative to saying "$5 donation" at the door. Putting this on your flier is a way of saying you want anyone who can pay to pay, but people who have a crappy allowance or low income can still come, too. It takes any possible elitism out of your event!

PASS THE HAT

Passing the hat is an alternative to charging at the door. Usually the person who organized the show, or a charismatic friend, gets up at some point in the proceedings and talks about how great the cause is, how great the band is, and why everybody should want to give a little money. Then a hat or some other container is passed around the room for people to put in however much they can afford. This is a great way to have a free show but still make a little money for touring or local bands. Get ready for some surprise donations that aren't necessarily monetary!

Putting together shows and promoting them for free isn't for everybody, but there is a certain breed of person who understands the value and beauty of a very cool all-ages event where everyone participating is happy and having a great time. As you organize shows for your town, you are doing a very cool thing for your community— bringing people together to play and listen to music on your terms, in your way. And you're doing it yourself!

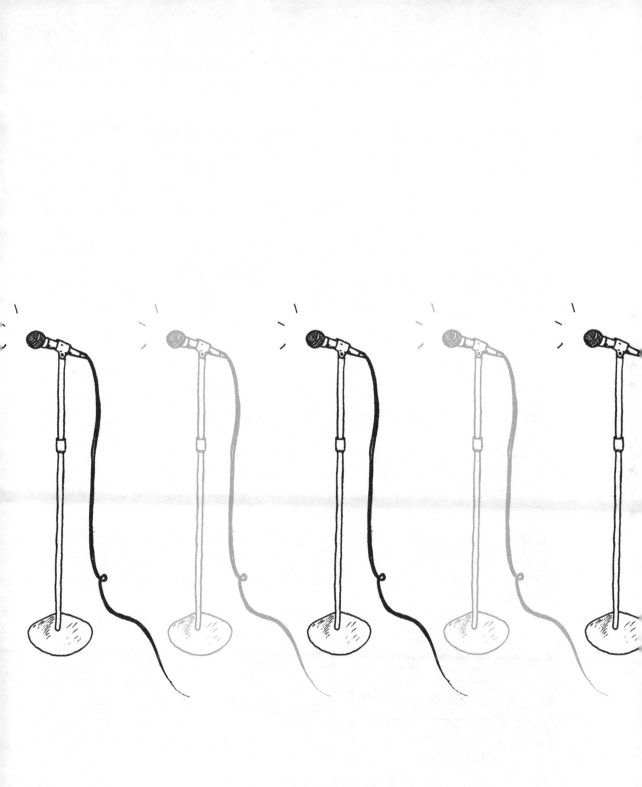

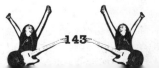

The Power OF COMMUNITY: hOW to FiND YOUR PEOPLE

BY NAZMIA JAMAL

I grew up in a little village in Wales and knew all of my neighbors. My family is large and sprawling and incredibly close. The religious community I grew up in is tight-knit, organized, and supportive. I should never have felt like I was out there on my own, but of course, strangely-dressed-bookworm-music-nerd that I was, that is exactly how I felt. In my small town I was one of the only Asians. At my girls' school, I was the only one who read the music press—and that is really where I began to find my own community.

In the early '90s, the back pages of the British music press revealed to me that I was not alone. In particular, the back pages of *Select* magazine were swarming with potential new friends, allies, and co-conspirators: people who had posted **zine** advertisements. I used to buy *Select*, a pack of envelopes, and a few books of stamps, and after I'd giggled over the three pages devoted to zines about Morrisey, I'd start sending off for zines. Soon I started writing one of my own, cutting and pasting at school and spending my lunch money on photocopying, staples, stamps, and, if I had any money left, maybe some fizzy bottles of cola.

Pretty much every morning of my life from 1996 to 1998 started with the arrival of a multitude of brightly colored envelopes filled with reviews, fliers, and trades of chocolate and records. It didn't matter that no one I knew liked bands like Bis or Kenickie or Gorky's Zygotic Munki. There were plenty of people out there who did. In among the letter writers were those who made excellent mix tapes, and in among those I made one very special connection: Maddy. Maddy sent me music that changed my life. Her tapes were filled with Bikini Kill, Huggy Bear, the Au Pairs, and, best of all, the Raincoats. I remember watching an interview with Beth Ditto a few years ago where she said something along the lines of, if your hometown isn't working out for you, "go and find your people." When Maddy started writing to me, I definitely found my people.

Letter writing helped me a lot when I was younger. These days, zine networks run by mail are much harder to tap into, and the places where you might find your people are going to be mainly online. E-mail lists, social networking sites, and message boards are all good places to find out about events that you are interested in or to find people who share your interests.

In 2001, I got involved with the group who was organizing Ladyfest London. During the organizing process we realized that a ready-made network was emerging for us through the piles of paper and cups of coffee at all the organizing meetings. These meetings were constantly punctuated with realizations that we'd all met before at shows, seen each other at clubs, been at the same parties, and written to each other as zine-producing teenagers.

For many of us, Ladyfest—the international coalition of music festivals that showcase female bands, promote skill-sharing and discussion about feminist issues, allow women to form organizing, self-sustaining, supportive communities of their own, and provide a space to celebrate women in all arenas of the arts—changed our lives. My first contact at Ladyfest London was the main organizer, who, although we'd never met, lived in the same house as Maddy, had read my zines, written to my best friend at school, and was on the same MA course as me.

For me, Ladyfest London offered a new way of expressing myself and of channeling my energy for community work and creativity. When the festival was over, I didn't want to let go of my new community; these amazing women who showed me how strong I am, that I deserve a voice and to be heard, that I am perfect as I am, and that there really is another, better way of doing things.

The community we'd set out to create with our festival was beautiful and newborn and needed sustaining, so we set up a collective to look after it. Together and in turns

the resulting Bakery Ladies put on gigs and events to gather our new family together. We joined other networks and worked with similar communities all over the United Kingdom. Not content with seeing each other at dark clubs and in loud spaces, we began to throw afternoon clubs; spaces where we could be together, a giant front room with tea and cakes and the all-important feeling of safety and belonging we often didn't get anywhere else.

Music was how we—the Ladyfesters, Bakery Ladies, homocrimers, Local Kids, FAG clubbers, Rock campers, and allies in the U.K.—came together. What started out as a Bikini Kill single, a Raincoats mix tape, a Sleater-Kinney obsession, a stack of Mr Lady CDs . . . has become a way of life for many of us. A shared love of *Hello Cuca* gives you a reason to talk to someone you've always wanted to be friends with. Friendships start on the basis that someone has a Bratmobile sticker on their car or is wearing an Electrelane T-shirt. But, of course, music on its own is not enough. The reason our community of music lovers has survived is because we've looked outside of our record bags and started realizing that we all have amazing things to offer. We can create as well as consume.

Born out of the Girls Rock and Ladies Rock Camps the first Ladies Rock! UK happened in London in 2007, marking an important coming of age for the community of people I found starting in the pages of *Select* six years before. Everyone pulled together to make the project work, and as I looked around at all the faces who'd come to Camp, I was aware that over time this group of people had stopped being just friends and people with the same taste in music and had become my family, my support network, and an inspiring, warm, creative community. Creating music, teaching, making art, setting up and running sound equipment, organizing—we've all been working together to give something back, reaching out to other people and making a community that is strong, supportive, and open, with music at its center.

I live in Stavanger, Norway, where there aren't many people who have heard of bands like Sleater-Kinney, Bikini Kill, or the Need. The first time I came to the Rock 'n' Roll Camp for Girls was in the summer of 2006. I had never really played music with anyone my age before, especially not any girls—just in my brother's cover band. It was the most freeing experience of my life, that first year as a camper, meeting young women my age who were interested in the same music I was, who wanted to play music as much as I did, and who exhibited such great passion for creating music. I formed a band at Camp and found myself playing guitar, jamming, writing music, even playing a solo. When the final rush from playing in front of hundreds of people at the showcase was over, all I could think about was taking all I had learned at Camp and making it happen at home.

I didn't know I had it in me.

Katelyn Mundal

How do you recognize and get away from a sketchy situation? Why is community important? What can you do to take care of yourself when you are onstage, in an audience, or going home after a show?

Your health and safety—mental, emotional, and physical—are the focus of this chapter. From the streets to the stage and even on the Internet, it's important to recognize what makes you feel safe and happy, and it is essential to build tools and support networks to promote the strength and health of your band, your community, and yourself.

WHY GiRLS-ONLY SPACE Is iMPORTanT

BY ELIZABETH VENABLE

I moved to Portland in the fall of 2003 knowing just a few people and looking for something to get involved in. The following summer, I heard about the Rock 'n' Roll Camp for Girls. A friend was in town to teach there and had an amazing recording of her guitar class—what sounded like twenty girls playing a Blondie song! I'd never heard such a sweet racket.

When I decided to try teaching at Rock Camp, I had to ask myself some questions. The Rock 'n' Roll Camp for Girls is a nonprofit organization run by women for girls and women. Men are encouraged to become involved and show support at some levels but not as instructors, and boys are not permitted to apply to any of its programs. Is this fair? Is this sexist? Prejudiced? Discriminatory?

These are questions that now, after working at Rock Camp for over three years, I've been asked time and time again in different forms. I'm sympathetic. It's taken some time for me to understand the answers. *Where am I supposed to take my son? Where is the Rock 'n' Roll Camp for Boys? Why a rock camp for girls? Why is this organization necessary?*

To begin addressing these concerns, let me start with my first experience with the organization. I went to a meeting at the Rock 'n' Roll Camp for Girls and sat in a room full of women, realizing that I'd never sat in a room full of women before. I've been the only woman in a room full of men plenty of times and one of few women at a rock show a million times. But this was all new to me.

I'd been a little wary going into that room, not wanting to be put into that box that defines its contents as being "girl power." Girl, girl, girl! Go girls!! For me, that can make it feel like I'm being surrounded by cheerleaders when what I need is a coach.

Part of me was extremely self-conscious. I knew nothing about this place or the people involved, yet I was afraid of being judged by the music I listened to, the music I played, my lack of teaching experience, my sexual preference, my womanhood! This was a wild observation for me, seeing new fears come into the light. It really made me think about myself and my place in society.

I was aware of going against the grain of a society that discourages people from joining together to find solutions to inequalities. I also felt a genuine comfort at that first Rock Camp meeting. I was sitting with a bunch of women involved in music and working for a common goal. I'd thought there might be some male bashing or some female bonding, but that's not why we were there. We were there to work together, to be part of this organization. We were there to learn and to teach.

Because we can't click our heels and make sexism go away, organizations like the Rock 'n' Roll Camp for Girls are necessary. Rock Camp gives girls and women support systems and opportunities they have historically been denied. By making knowledge and information accessible, and providing a safe space for girls and women, Rock Camp is a key element in bringing about necessary social change.

..testimonial...

I think my gender isolation is a large influence on my decision to come back, year after year. The fact that no other male has volunteered during the four years I've been here is a testament to the necessity of Rock Camp. Many times I have thought, or heard from others, how great it would be if this camp weren't necessary; if girl bands and boy bands garnered equal respect in the musical community; if the genders mixed in music; if the differences were respected, not exploited for corporate bigwigs.

Nathan Kenney

HOW TO
spiN the
web
(ANd NOT
GeT STUCK)

BY CHELSEY JOHNSON

The Internet! It can be your best friend; it can be your worst enemy—no, wait. I take that back. It will never replace your best friend, nor single-handedly attempt to destroy you. Start again: The Internet! It can be your good buddy who knows all the right people, and steps in to help when you need it; it can be that slack older brother reclined on the basement couch eating chips and doing nothing productive; it can be that weird old guy you see hanging out across the street from the school who you want to stay far, far away from. However you look at it, the Internet is a pretty essential part of how we make and learn about and hear new music. Here's how to make it work for you—and how to protect yourself and your bandmates in a space that doesn't provide the physical or informational boundaries of the real world.

Where to Start

Look at the websites of some of your favorite bands, or any bands, really. What do you like about their sites? What annoys you or seems unnecessary? What features or content do you wish their sites had that they don't? What looks good? What are some of the coolest details? Write down notes! And bookmark the pages you like best—if you or one of your bandmates or friends is HTML-savvy, you can click "view source code" and see how they made it look and work the way they did.

Creating Your Site

Whether it's a social networking page (such as MySpace or Facebook) or www.yourawesomebandname.com, keep in mind that the whole point of a website is to *communicate information* about your band. Design it to the hilt if that's your thing, but keep it clean, readable, and easy to navigate. A clear, simple, easy-to-read site is way more effective than a super-tricked-out, overly busy, flashing site that induces headaches and/or seizures. You want a site that makes people want to read on, not shield their eyes, cover their ears, or bang their heads on the keyboard in frustration. Fortunately, this is pretty simple. Check out these do's and don'ts.

YES! INCLUDE:

- Text that is large enough to read, presented in a normal, readable font, and easy on the eyes.
- Contact info so people who are interested in booking you or interviewing you know how to reach you.
- Set up an alternate e-mail address that's for band-related things only, and check that regularly. If you receive a lot of stuff by mail, you might want to get a post office box.
- Pictures of your band in action, playing. A good clear photo of your band that could be reprinted in a newspaper or magazine—one that's 300 dpi, if possible.
- Upcoming shows. (Plus you can list who you've played with in the past, especially if you've opened or played with bands with some name recognition.)
- Post a couple of MP3s if you've recorded your stuff.

NO! DO NOT INCLUDE:

- ▶ Neon text on bright patterned backgrounds, hyperactive blinking/flashing text—you get the idea.
- ▶ Your home address.
- ▶ Your actual personal e-mail address (spambots will scoop it up).
- ▶ Your phone number.
- ▶ Pictures of yourself doing anything that might come back to haunt you when you run for president some day.
- ▶ Remember, the Internet is PUBLIC. If you wouldn't say it or show it to an auditorium full of people—including, say, your grandmother—don't post it on the Internet. When in doubt, show restraint. Why? Well, read on.

Fending Off the Creeps, a.k.a. Why and How to Play It Safe

I am sorry to say this, but if you are a girl, at some point you will have to deal with creeps. This is no fault of your own. You are the light, and creeps are moths. This does not mean you should stop shining. Just know how to swat away the (generally, though not always, male) people who might make you feel icky and/or try to cross your path.

Creeps may be obviously pathetic and nasty, or they may come across as charming and sweet. They can appear in the form of a grown-up who seems a bit *too* interested in you, or in the form of a sketchy promoter who's trying to get you to play a show where you have to buy a block of tickets to resell (the notorious pay-to-play scam—don't do this), or in the form of someone dangling a big wad of cash if only you'll sign away your firstborn on the dotted line. Creeps, alas, thrive on the Internet, and try to use it to their advantage. Here are some tips to keep them out of your life—some bug-zapping advice, if you will.

1. First of all, keep your personal life personal.

As soon as you start recording and releasing things and playing shows, you're taking a step into public life. This is exciting—a lot of the joy of making music is bringing it out into the world and playing it with and for other people. It's really rewarding and exciting when your band gets recognized and people start to know who you are.

There's a payoff, though—maybe it's just to a miniscule degree, but it can balloon pretty quickly if your music catches on, even on a small scale—and that is that once

you step into public life, people become interested in your private life. Some people don't care what their favorite musicians do for fun, if they have a boyfriend/girlfriend, what their past is, or whatever—but some people are fanatically devoted to learning every detail of what their hero eats for breakfast, their favorite color, where they hang out, where they live, and what is the quickest route to get there.

As recent articles can attest, it's shockingly easy to track someone via their online profiles. A total stranger can figure out pretty quickly where you go to school, what extracurricular activities you do, who your friends are, what you look like offstage, what's going on in your life, and where you hang out. Here are some ways to help prevent this:

➡ Make your personal profiles friends-only.

➡ Don't put your personal profile as a top friend on your band's page. Instead, put up friends' bands, other bands you like, supportive friends and organizations, etc.

➡ Skip your last name, or adopt a stage name. Keep your last name off of your account settings—use an initial, for example. This makes it tougher for someone outside your trusty friend network to dig you up on a random search. You might also want to consider the great tradition of adopting a stage name, like everyone from the Ramones to the Wu-Tang Clan to Salt 'n' Pepa have done. Or you can do as the girls in Smoosh have done and forgo last names altogether—they just go by Asya and Chloe to protect their family's identity and privacy.

➡ Be careful about what you blog about publicly. If you keep an online journal or blog, keep your personal life friends-only.

2. You don't have to be everyone's friend.

On the Rock 'n' Roll Camp for Girls social networking sites, we get friend requests every single day from people who have no idea who we are or what we do, and don't even really care—sometimes, in fact, they turn out to be people who seem to embody the exact *opposite* of our mission. These are the ones who are easy to spot: they have only thong-clad bikini models in their top 8, they are a fake profile advertising a web cam and some gift cards, they are a forty-eight-year-old man in Belgium with a page background of spinning marijuana leaves, or they are an Arkansas dude-metal band waving a confederate flag. Then there are a zillion bands who have six thousand friends and apparently nothing to do with girls or feminism—they just want more numbers.

You are absolutely entitled to hit DENY. It's not going to destroy the self-esteem of one Jeff in Kansas if you don't friend him. (And if it does, he's got bigger problems to worry about.) Also, think about this: Is it more important to you to have six thousand "friends" who have no idea who you are or care what you do, or to have a couple hundred contacts who are genuinely interested in your music? It's up to you, but we personally go with the latter, and only friend people who actually care about who we are and what we do.

3. Trust your gut feeling.

If you are getting a weird vibe from someone, even if it's just via an e-mail exchange, even if you can't find something overtly suspicious about them, don't doubt yourself. Trust your instincts, and remember, *you* call the shots about who you respond to and who you avoid. Which leads to . . .

4. You can choose to write back—or not.

Chances are, most of the messages you get from people are going to be nice. Corresponding with like-minded music lovers can be incredibly rewarding and can forge genuine friendships and connections. And attention is flattering.

But sometimes people's motives are not really about appreciating your art. If you feel suspicious or weird about the tone or intent of someone who's writing you, you don't have to write back at all. This sounds obvious, right? But it's crazy how as girls we have this expectation that we're always supposed to be "nice" and polite and concerned about hurting people's feelings. If someone is contacting you inappropriately, you have every right to:

➽ ignore them completely, and/or
➽ politely discontinue contact, and/or
➽ clearly and firmly tell them to cut it out, and/or
➽ notify a trusted adult and/or the authorities.

People don't like being rejected and sometimes will react strongly. Don't get caught up in it. Respond calmly and firmly, or ignore them.

5. If someone is weirding you out, tell someone else—talk about it with your bandmates, and tell a trusted adult in your life.

Don't think, "Oh, it's just me," or worry that you're being paranoid or a baby. You might find out that someone else in your band is experiencing something similar.

6. As a general rule, save all correspondence.

Save all your e-mail and message exchanges—even your IMs and chats, if you can. On the positive side, this helps you keep track of who your friends and fans are for future networking and/or touring, and on the protective side, it means that you have evidence on your side if a situation ever gets out of hand.

So, remember: The Internet is a good way to communicate about your music and make connections with people who appreciate and support it. Just keep in mind to remain focused on the artistic and professional purposes, and save the majority of yourself for *you.* You already put so much of your thoughts and feelings into your art— so outside of your music, it's smart to be protective of your true self and your privacy, in order to keep control of your life, your sense of self, and your personal safety.

And finally, always remember, no matter how friends-only or private you think you're being, THE INTERNET HAS NO SECRETS. Never post anything that you would not want to come back to haunt you when you run for president—or become the rock 'n' roll hero of the next generation of girls.

SELF-DEFENSE

JODI DARBY

Community responses to violence against women are the inspiration for the self-defense curriculum taught at the Rock 'n' Roll Camp for Girls. In fact, the existence of the Rock 'n' Roll Camp for Girls is itself a form of self-defense. Rock Camp works to create a web of support and safety for girls and young women with the hope that every girl who participates in our programs becomes ready and able to stand up for and defend herself, her friends, and her community.

I grew up in the suburbs of Washington DC, and started going to punk shows in the mid to late '80s. It was a time when young people were angry about the state of the union and disillusioned with Reagan's cold war militarization and rampant corruption in the nation's capital.

Punk in DC was loud and aggressive and dominated by men. Riot Grrrl, the movement to make punk shows less male-dominated, had yet to hit its stride, and women at punk shows mostly hung out in the back of the room. My experience was one of frustration; I wanted nothing more than to fling myself into the pit—its stinking mass of sweaty bodies and flailing elbows—but I knew that I risked getting my head taken off by some guy in jump boots.

It was around this time that I began to think seriously about self-defense. My interest in the topic came not from poring over feminist theory or having close calls in the street, but from a basic desire to take up space in a place that I felt intrinsically forbidden to enter.

I studied self-defense to learn proper stance and balance so that I wouldn't end up on the floor at hardcore shows. I learned to practice assertive body language and eye contact. And, before learning more subtle skills like strikes and targets, I learned how to throw a well-timed punch.

Being a girl at punk shows taught me to take up the space that was mine to take up, to not step aside and give away my power. It taught me hard and fast lessons on boundaries, non-verbal communication, and the benefits of walking away from an unsafe situation.

As I grew older, self-defense became part of my response to the violence against women and girls that is entrenched in our society. In my early twenties, I watched friends scatter to different parts of the country in pursuit of freedom. Some of my friends moved because of music, trekking to San Francisco, Seattle, or Olympia in hopes of finding community among the musicians there. I began hearing disturbing stories from my far-flung friends—stories of assaults or attempted assaults, violence at the hands of their partners, and of dates gone wrong due to forceful breaches of consent. I wasn't naive enough to think that this was a new phenomenon; this violence and sexual aggression had touched many people that I cared about. I understood it as a problem deeply imbedded in the psyche of our culture. I realized I was being forced to make decisions based on the threat of violence. These decisions affected my freedom of movement, and this lack of freedom was causing me to become nervous, mistrustful, paranoid, and, finally, angry. My safety, or lack thereof, impacted my life every day.

In 1993, Mia Zapata, the singer for the Gits, a respected and much-loved woman in Seattle's punk community, was raped and murdered. This terrible event reverberated through communities of women and reminded us all that no matter how spirited and strong we might be, we are all potential victims of violent crimes.

Women in the punk community pooled their anger and responded creatively to this violence. San Francisco's Tribe 8's song "Frat Pig" and Seven Year Bitch's "Dead Men Don't Rape" became anthems to the frustration that was being felt coast to coast. Back in DC, Bikini Kill's Kathleen Hanna declared, "Revolution, girl style—NOW!" and in Seattle, local artists and musicians banded together to create Home Alive, a resource center that taught various methods of self-defense and an option-based antiviolence curriculum.

In 1995, I began studying self-defense in earnest. For me, devoting time to these skills served several purposes. It helped me to feel safer and more powerful in my life. It also helped to temper the anger I felt in response to seeing friends and loved ones victimized. It gave me the opportunity to turn that anger into energy, to create something positive out of a negative situation.

Self-defense education gave me two important methods to address the threat of violence: awareness and fighting back.

The first step in defending yourself is becoming aware of your surroundings. It's important to learn to present ourselves as "hard targets"—making ourselves appear confident and aware, in spite of how we might actually be feeling at the time.

Imply confidence in many ways: for starters, look straight ahead rather than at the ground, make sure your stance is stable, and keep your knees slightly bent so that you aren't easily set off balance.

For a simple exercise based in a common real-life situation, pretend to be standing at the bus stop. First, stand with one leg crossed over the other and pretend your hands are busy, maybe turning the pages of a magazine. Pretend you are listening to your iPod. Your eyes are lowered, and you are concentrating on your reading.

At this point, your senses are compromised. You are unable to hear or see if someone is moving toward you. You will be taken completely off guard if someone taps you on the shoulder. Your stance is not solid, and chances are you will lose your balance if someone were to push you. Finally, since your arms are busy, you will not be able to use them to defend yourself, either by blocking a strike or throwing one yourself.

Now try this: Stand with your legs about shoulder width apart and with your knees slightly bent. Keep your head up and pay attention to where you are. If you are on a street with little light, pay attention to where the closest well-lit street is. That way, if you need to run to safety, you will already know which way to go. If it is late at night, locate a late-night establishment nearby, a place where you could head for help. If you

are indoors, pay attention to where the exits are. While you are in your solid stance and aware of your surroundings, practice assertive body language, look around, keep your hands free and loose at your sides.

Taking up space is important and there is a distinct difference between assertive and aggressive behavior. When you are in a group of people, pay attention to who those people are. You don't have to engage everybody in a staring contest, but a healthy awareness of the people around you is important. If you notice someone who seems sketchy or unsafe to you, fixing that person with a nice, solid gaze can be an assertive move that doesn't necessarily come across as a provocation. I call it my " I could pick you out of a police lineup" look. Making yourself appear confident makes you more aware of the space you occupy, and of the other people in that space.

Intuition is another aspect of awareness. Intuition is also called "gut feeling," a feeling of unease or discomfort with certain situations or around certain people. Ever heard someone say, "I just get a bad feeling about that person . . ."? That's intuition in action. Our intuition is just as smart as our brains and is a powerful tool in keeping ourselves safe. As girls and women, we are told to be polite and friendly at all times. So, what do you do when you are approached by somebody— whether it is a stranger asking you for the time, the boy at school who has a crush on you, or a relative who asks for too many hugs—and your "gut feeling" tells you to stay away? You have every right to communicate in an assertive manner in order to protect yourself. Following your intuition is much more important than being polite. Following your intuition may save your life.

Your voice is another important tool for keeping yourself safe. You can use your voice to name behaviors that are making you feel weird and you can tell someone what you want him or her to do—for example, "You're standing too close. Please take a step back."

If a person is angry and on the verge of using violence, they are not thinking clearly and, as a result, might not be hearing you. You can use your voice to de-escalate, or calm down a situation. Talk in a relaxed voice, repeat yourself, and incorporate a non-confrontational stance—open hands and eye contact—to calm a situation down. For example, "It's okay. I don't want any trouble. It's okay. I don't want any trouble." Repeating yourself in this way is a tactic called "broken record" and it can be used when someone is angry and having a hard time hearing what you are saying. Using the broken record will help your message get through.

If a situation continues to escalate, you can use your voice to draw attention to yourself and to call for help. You can use a firm, loud, and angry tone to tell the potential attacker to back off.

Practice using your voice to give commands or to yell "NO!" When you yell, yell from your diaphragm, down near your belly—it gives you more power and it also keeps you breathing. Practice using a serious voice and matching your tone with the expression on your face. Pretend you're a lion or a grizzly bear and roar and growl to your heart's content.

Girls are often told to keep quiet, that yelling or speaking in a commanding way is not acceptable. But the truth is, your voice is a powerful tool that is just as important and useful in protecting yourself as it is for making beautiful sounds.

If using your voice to make demands or to calm down a situation doesn't work, your last resort is to fight. If you have made the decision to fight, it is important to commit yourself to fighting 100 percent. In fighting 100 percent you are fighting in a focused and tactical way. There is a big difference between fighting and struggling. When you struggle, you don't use your energy in strategic ways and you may end up exhausting yourself.

Fighting means identifying targets that will incapacitate your attacker so that you can get away to safety. Fighting also means that when you strike those targets on your attacker, you are striking as hard as you possibly can, in an attempt to inflict the most damage. Remember: You could be fighting for your life.

The basic targets on a human body are the eyes, nose, throat, groin, and knees. These body parts are exceptionally vulnerable.

Eyes—A person can work out at the gym ten hours a day and still be completely incapacitated by a strike to the eye. If you've ever gotten an eyelash or a piece of dust in your eye you know what I mean.

Nose—The palm of the hand to the base of the nose is a very effective and painful strike.

Throat—Two fingers to the top part of the throat, just above the collarbone, can catch your attacker off guard and buy yourself some time.

Groin—The groin is a sensitive spot for both men and women. A swift kick to the crotch can bring your attacker to his knees.

Knees—No matter how big and strong a person is, their knees only bend in one direction. If you blow out their knee they aren't going to chase after you.

So, if you feel like you would be powerless against an attacker, think again. Remember: YOU CAN DEFEND YOURSELF AND YOU ARE WORTH DEFENDING.

Being politically aware of violence means taking a critical look at societal responses to that violence. On television and in movies we are presented with images and narratives of violence that portray women as passive victims. Rarely are we presented with images of regular women (as opposed to female superheroes or Anime avatars) fighting back. It's not surprising that the constant threat and portrayal of violence has created a climate of fear where many women don't believe they have options for dealing with violence. Our class is all about options, deciding for ourselves how we take care of ourselves, and never, ever, *ever* blaming ourselves for an attack.

Let's deconstruct some myths. By teaching verbal self-defense skills that fit a range of situations, we help girls assert their boundaries. We generate conversation between young people about these myths and others:

Myth #1: Stranger Danger—the idea that the person whom you should fear most is the stranger skulking behind the dumpster.

Truth: Many assaults occur at the hands of friends, relatives, and intimate partners.

Myth #2: Girls and women are responsible for their safety by watching what they wear, where and when they walk, and how they present themselves.

Truth: Every person has the right to wear what she chooses, walk where she wants to go, and present herself as who she is. We are all responsible for keeping each other safe.

Myth #3: Women "ask for" sexual and physical assault.

Truth: No person is ever asking to be assaulted.

Self-defense must be a single part of a larger project. We understand that self-defense will not eradicate sexual and physical violence against women and girls, but in studying self-defense we challenge the system that allows violence to continue. We challenge the system that creates fear of performing on a stage, fear of using our voices, fear of being loud and of being powerful. Through self-defense, we challenge the assumption that girls are weak, and we reinforce the idea that not only can we defend ourselves, but that we are *worth* defending.

And if self-defense helps you feel more powerful in the mosh pit, all the better.

Punk Rock Aerobics

BY HILKEN MANCINI
AND MAURA JASPER

Punk Rock Aerobics (PRA) is an unlikely combination of punk and fitness born out of a rejection of the conventional workout options. We offer no fitness "regime" and we mandate no diets. We have no interest in telling anyone how to live her life, and we certainly don't want you to try and fit into anything.

PRA is about getting off your butt, having fun, and feeling good. Pursuing physical well-being can be as cool as mastering that sick guitar-tapping lick. It doesn't have to mean signing up to be an automaton on a Stairmaster, or turning into a self-obsessed lame brain whose only concern is fitting into a size zero pair of brand-name pants. We're here to make you realize you can obtain the "raw power" to get in shape, and that it can be a really cool time. Getting fit can be fun—but it can also be a great way to vent all your angst and frustration out at the world. Sometimes screaming into the microphone or pounding on the snare just isn't enough. A few brave minutes of exercise a day can leave you with a self-confidence that no one will mess with—and we all know that nothing is better than hanging tough and being able to roughhouse with the best of 'em.

Punk Rock Aerobics is a totally DIY workout created by a couple of out-of-shape music lovers. The combination of a formal exercise program and punk rock may sound like the dumbest thing you've ever heard. Let's face it, punk has always been about looking around at the existing options and saying, "No, thanks." Punks started their own bands and, when they couldn't get their records pressed by major music labels, they started their own labels.

Punk Rock Aerobics was born out of this tradition—starting PRA was like starting a band without knowing how to play an instrument. We knew what we wanted and, more important, what we didn't want; we had a vision. We didn't want to go to a class that played music that sucked. We wanted a class that wasn't in a gym with fluorescent lighting and mirrors, but in a space where it was more than okay to have zero coordination. Where it was cool to wear cheap sneakers and shorts from Goodwill, and where we wouldn't be held to conventional standards of beauty. Most important: We wanted it to be fun to get in shape. We didn't want to have to fit ourselves into what was being offered to us, or what was already there. That's when we realized we had to pave the road ourselves.

Punk Rock Aerobics shares a lot with the ideas and ideals of RnRC4G, and probably with you, too! Hatching an idea with like-minded people and working hard to turn those ideas into a reality is a great feat. But one thing about Punk Rock Aerobics that you may not be so interested in yet may be the whole "getting in shape" part. After all, you want to rock out, not hulk out! But before you completely blow us off, you may need to hear why it's important to be in shape and why you need to get started early. By incorporating these skills now, you can have them for the rest of your life. So let's just get down to the brass tacks (but also check out the Resources section on page 181).

Prepare and Take Care

When you want to rock "full-metal jacket" style, we all know the ammunition is you, your instrument, and the gear you use to play it. It's important for all of these things to be in primo shape so you can be the best you can be. The same way you prepare and take care of your equipment is the same way you need to treat yourself. You know you won't be able to play through your amp if you never maintain it, or let the tubes burn out. If you never keep up your drum kit by tuning it, or never change the heads, it will just sound dead when you play it (unless you're Charlie Watts). If you never put

your cords and cables away properly and just leave them on the floor and let them ball up into a tangled mess, they will just stop working eventually, right? Well, it's the same thing with your body. If you can't really commit to any sort of regular exercise, eventually you will notice an atrophy that will set in and only get worse as you grow older. So before you set your watch to snooze, you may want to read on. You'll be thanking us when it comes time to lug your amp around.

Exercise increases the number and size of blood vessels, lowering blood pressure and increasing lung capacity. Exercise will help those of you who "play the microphone" by singing in front of a loud band to project louder and hold notes for longer. Supporting your notes from someplace other than your throat is important for more reasons than just to protect your vocal cords. If you are in shape you will be able to take deeper breaths, your stomach muscles will be stronger, and your diaphragm will have more support, thereby allowing you to attain the breath control you've only dreamed about. Whether you are screaming, singing, or belting it out, you'll be on top of your game and using the foundation that only a healthy body can give.

Exercise also builds greater bone density. Bones grow in response to working muscle mass. This means exercise can improve posture, so even if you were borrowing the heaviest of guitars from Camp, you won't slouch à la Keith Richards. You will be able to straighten your back and open up your shoulders. This posture may not seem ultra cool to you, but caving in over your instrument every day can lead to back and neck pain (and eventually to all kinds of musculoskeletal ailments). Playing the bass, which is a heavier instrument, requires the same, if not more, support. Either way, being able to show off your strong shoulders as you shred wildly sounds like a better idea than any to us.

Exercise will also improve your balance and coordination while increasing your range of motion, so drummers, listen up! We all know how extremely physical and important your role is. The amount of coordination you need to hold the band together, while keeping a dynamic approach, can be more than exhausting.

And for everyone who performs, come showtime, you may be so nervous that you are afraid you might pass out or have a heart attack. But with the increased endurance you've achieved by exercising, your heart will be pumping blood with ease, your anxiety and tension will be released (or at least reduced!), and you'll be able to pull off a stage-diving performance like a pro. You may even go out after the show and steal the dance floor out from everyone around you. This is what being in shape can do for you. Who wouldn't want to be like that?

In general, whichever instrument(s) you play, you want to make sure that you are in the best of shape to execute any of the moves you'll need! There are tons more important facts—we haven't even given you the half of it. If we went on to tell you more—from exercise being a miraculous antidepressant to increasing resistance to all kinds of illness—well, you'd think it almost sounds like a scam. So now you know why it's important to be in shape as a rocker, and also why it's "punk rock" the way we like to do it.

So here's where the fun part comes in . . .

Ready, Steady, Go

The following exercises are just a taste of what a Punk Rock Aerobics class can really be like. We start with slow warm-up moves (Lo-Fi) and move on to higher-impact ones (Hi-Fi). The first three are great for warming up before a show or practice, so you won't end up sprained or strained. The last three are more high impact and may be fun to have a solo dance party in your bedroom with, or pull them out in a crowd and impress your bandmates and friends. You can whip these off in no time and you'll be "loose"—Iggy style—for whatever comes your way. Don't worry if you're doing it "right." Just have fun. If you are moving and having a good time doing it, you're on the right track. That's what it's all about.

LO-FI MOVES

Once you have these down, try running them in succession—you'll feel like a real champ!

Deltoid Void
Feel like your arms have an uncontrollable urge.
1. Stand facing straight ahead.
2. Bring your left arm up sideways toward the midline of your body.
3. Swing your raised left arm horizontally across your body and grab it behind your upper arm with your right hand. Keep your left arm extended.
4. Pulling your extended left arm gently to the right, hold it to your chest with your right hand. Turn and look to the left. Hold for 10 seconds.
5. Release and repeat on other side, stretching your right arm to the left and looking to the right.
6. Do this twice on each side.

Neck-Breaka

As you roll your head, listen for that crackling sound . . . the sound of excessive headbanging to Ozzy.

1. Stand facing straight ahead, with your feet shoulder width apart.
2. Drop your chin down to your chest.
3. Keeping your chin down close to your body, roll your neck from shoulder to shoulder in a smooth, controlled motion, 180 degrees.
4. Roll your neck from side to side.
5. Rest and repeat.

Ripped T-shirt Stretch

You knew there was a reason you never threw away that circa 2001 summer camp T-shirt.

1. Stand facing straight ahead.
2. With the ripped T-shirt in your right hand, lift it up and over your head and bend it back behind your head.
3. Bend your left arm behind your back and bring it up so it can reach and grasp onto the other end of the ripped T-shirt. Hold for 10 seconds.
4. Slowly move your hands as close together as possible by crawling them up or down the T-shirt. Hold for 10 seconds.
5. Switch sides and repeat with your other arm over your head.

Tip: The goal is to have your hands move closer and closer every time until they eventually touch. This is hard and takes a lot of flexibility. You need to work up to it. Don't jump into this one; it's a good one when your body has warmed up a bit, or maybe even after you've worked out.

HI-FI MOVES

Skank

For this one, channel those skinheads from the pit and make it as aggressive as you can. If you're familiar with the drawing of the punk kid on Circle Jerks records, imitate him and you'll be all set.

1. Make fists with your hands. Move your arms and legs as if marching in place.
2. Make the movements big and aggressive, bringing your arms and knees up much higher.
3. Jump with each swing of the arms and legs.
4. Rock your head back and forth.

Wack-Jack

A jumping jack, only wacked; don't think about it, just shut up and do as we say.

1. Stand facing straight ahead, then jump both your feet out to the sides (as you would for a regular jumping jack).
2. As both your legs go out to the sides, lift your upper arms out to your sides, elbows bent and hands facing down.
3. Jump, and cross your feet and arms in, one in front of the other.
4. Jump back out and in again (crossing your arms and feet the other way).

Tip: Remember when you jump out to the side, your knees should never completely straighten. You could hurt your knees that way, and the last thing you want to do is to explain to your friends that you injured yourself while doing a wack-jack.

You Be the Star Air Guitar

This is the chance we know you've been waiting for. It's time to find your inner guitar god and break out the licks. We like to throw in Pete Townsend "windmills" for added cardio kick, but you may have a favorite shredder move of your own. After all, personal style is the key to a winning air guitar performance.

1. Stand in a lunging position with your left knee centered over your toes, right leg back straight.
2. Raise your left arm straight out at your side (as if you were holding the neck of a guitar).
3. Swing your right arm in a circle, making a windmill. As you swing the arm, kick your right leg straight out with it.
4. Jump up and down on your left leg for a count of 4.
5. Turn to your right and do this on your right side.

Tip: We jump to a count of 4, but if another count works better in the song you choose, modify accordingly.

Neck-Breaka

Deltoid Void

Ripped T-shirt Stretch

Wack-Jack

Skank

You Be the Star Air Guitar

GLOSSARY

A

Acoustic—An instrument or setup that does not use electricity.

Action—On a guitar, the distance between the fret board and the strings.

Agent—*See* Booking agent

All-ages—A label used to describe an event appropriate for and open to a person of any age.

Amp/amplifier—A device used to make sound louder.

Analog—Sound that is captured, stored, and processed in a non-digital medium. Analog formats include records and tapes. *See also* Digital.

Arpeggio—Three or more notes of a chord played as a series of single notes.

Arrange—To decide the order of the parts (verse, chorus, bridge) in a song.

Arrangement—The structure of a song, including the order of the parts and how many times those parts are repeated.

B

B-side—Side two of a vinyl record; usually refers to a 7-inch single. Record companies used to try to put a hit song on side one, and a song they didn't expect to be as popular on side two.

Band coach—A person at Rock Camp who helps a band with their arrangements, instrumentation, and communication.

Bar—Also called *measure*. A unit of time (often four beats) expressed musically. *See also* Time signature.

Barré chords—These are chords played on a guitar that require the index finger to lay across the fret board and press three, four, or strings at a time.

Basic tracks—The first tracks in a recording, usually rhythm tracks. Basic tracks are what the different instruments and voices on a recording play to when recording their parts.

Benefit show—An event that raises money for a cause, also called a *fundraiser.* Typically bands will play for free and you can offer a sliding scale at the door. Sometimes venues will offer the space for a cut rate or free to support the cause as well. If you are booking the show and bands, you get to determine if *all* or part of the proceeds go toward the cause. You can choose to cover your costs or donate them to the cause as well. Make sure everyone knows it's a benefit!

Bill—The lineup of bands or other performers who will be performing at a show.

Bleed—Usually undesirable, the sound of an instrument or voice being picked up by the mic for another instrument during a live recording.

Booker—A person who works for a venue scheduling bands and solo artists.

Booking agent—A person who works for a band or performer to get them shows.

Booking—The process of picking the time and date of a show, worked from the band and the venue side.

BPM—Beats per minute; a unit of measure often used when making beats or when DJing to match records.

Breakdown—*See* Bridge.

Bridge—The part in a song where an entirely new melody is introduced, often also the place where you will hear a "solo" of the guitar/sax/nose flute sort. Also called *Breakdown*.

Busking—Performing on the street for tips.

C

Cable/cord—The long, skinny cord used to play an instrument or mic into an amp, or a PA head into the speakers.

Calendar listing—A mention of a show in the calendar section of a publication.

Chest voice—Singing that originates in the chest cavity, not the skull and nasal cavities, usually in the lower range of the voice. *See also* Head voice.

Chord—A group of two or more notes played at once.

Chord progression—A sequence of chords.

Chorus—The catchy theme of the song, usually repeated.

Club—Short for nightclub; a smaller venue, often a bar.

Combo amp—A cabinet containing an amp head and a speaker.

Cover charge—The cost of getting into a show.

Credits—Information on the cover or insert of a record or CD telling who played, engineered, produced, etc., the recordings.

Crescendo—A buildup of volume and intensity in music.

D

Demo—A lo-fi recording, or demonstration, of your work, made for the purpose of giving away to bookers and record labels to impress them and get the opportunity to work with them.

D.I. box—An electronic device used to modify the signal sent from an instrument to the PA. *D.I.* stands for *direct input* or *direct injection*.

Digital—Sound or other data as binary numbers (1s and 0s) used to process, transmit, and store information on a computer or a CD. *See also* Analog.

Distro—Short for *distribution*. A distro is responsible for stocking records and delivering them to record stores or through the mail.

DIY—Do It Yourself! This expression refers to an aesthetic, or values system, as well as an approach to getting things done.

Door—This refers to 1) the time your venue will open the door to let paying people in, and 2) how much you make at the end of the night. For example: "Last show, doors were at 7 P.M., the first band started at 7:30, and we made $150 at the door."

Door person—The person who takes money as people come in to a show. Often, a door person ink-stamps a unique symbol on each person's hand after they pay their cover so she can see who has already been in, and (usually) let them go in and out.

Door split/splitting the door—An agreement between the venue and the person organizing the show to establish how to share the money made at the door. A common door split is in favor of the organizer. A 50/50 split is also common. If you have a 60/40 split in your favor and you make $100 at the door, you get $60 and the venue gets $40. Sometimes venues will ask for a flat rate and then a split, such as $50

up front and then a 70/30 split of the door. In general, you should make more money than the venue. If the venue ends up costing more than the show makes, consider a different venue.

Downstroke—A downward strum of hand, fingers, or pick over the strings of a guitar or similar instrument.

dpi—*Dots per inch,* or a measure of the resolution of a photo.

Draw—The term for how many people come to see a specific band or support a specific cause. If there is a band with a good, or big, draw, they typically go last under the logic that most people will stick around for the whole show waiting for the popular band, thereby making the energy higher, giving the club a chance to make more money, and getting greener bands exposure.

Drone—A repeated tone or note over which a melody is played.

Drum machine—A device for producing beats, often found on a keyboard or a computer.

Drum notation—Written music for drums.

Dynamics—Softness and loudness in music.

E

Echo box—An effects box that simulates the sound of an echo. *Echo* is a sound that has a delay of 35 milli-seconds or more.

Effects—Refers to the many different ways to modify a signal. Examples include *flange, chorus, reverb,* and *delay.*

Effects pedal—An onstage device that can be triggered with the feet, used to generate effects.

Electronic—Sounds that are created and/or controlled digitally.

EQ—Short for *equalization*, or the balance of the high, mid, and low ranges of live or recorded sound. *See also* Range.

EQing—The term for making adjustments to the sound, either with the tone knobs on your amplifier or instrument (or other effects pedals) while playing, or with the addition of electronic components in the recording studio.

F

Fader—The squarish knob that slides up and down to control the volume on certain types of mixing boards.

Falsetto—Singing in a very high voice; usually refers to male voices.

Fanzine—*See* Zine.

Feedback—The howling, screaming, reverberating sound of a mic or electric guitar picking itself up over and over. Sometimes this is a good thing, sometimes it is very painful.

Fifth—A note that is five notes higher up the music alphabet than your starting note.

Flat fee—A sum of money guaranteed as payment to a band for playing a show. *See also* Guarantee.

Fliers—Homemade advertisements to be posted in public places to spread the word and give vital information about a show. A flier is usually 8½-by-11-inch paper that clearly conveys the bill, time, location name and address, cost, and date of the show.

4-track—A recording machine that allows the user to record on four separate tracks.

4/4—Refers to music that has four beats to a bar where the quarter note gets the beat. *See also* Time signature.

Frequency—In music, the number of sound waves or vibrations per second, a setting used to create or change the tone of an electric instrument, speaker, amplifier, etc.

G

Gain—Signal level. The control for how much signal is sent to an amplifier.

Gig—Slang for *show* or *performance.*

Guarantee—A set fee that some bands, often those with a large draw or significant expenses, charge to play. Bands who require a guarantee often will waive or lower their fee if the show is a benefit they really believe in.

Guest list—A list of people who are invited by the band or show organizers to get in free. It is customary for each bandmember to get one guest who doesn't have to pay the cover, but you as the organizer can decide. The guest list is often just called "the List."

H

Handbill—A small flier, sized to be convenient and affordable to hand out freely. A common technique is to shrink down a poster or flier so that it fits four to an 8½-by-11-inch page.

Harmonies—Notes and tunes played or sung along a melody.

Harmonize—To play or sing any combination of notes that move in ryhthm with the melody line but are not exactly the same pitch as the melody.

Headliner—The band, performer, or act that will play last on the bill and usually has the biggest draw. The headliner usually has the most fans, supportive friends, largest family in attendance, or has played a lot of shows so people know who they are. One thing's for sure—you don't *need* a headliner to put on a show, but whoever plays last is considered the headliner whether they have a draw or not. Also used as a verb, to headline.

Head voice—Singing in the high range of a voice where the tone is coming from within the skull and nasal cavities, not the chest. *See also* Chest voice.

Hi-fi—Stands for *high fidelity,* refers to sounds that are clear and clean. *See also* Lo-fi.

Hook—A catchy riff or tune. The defining phrase of a song that gets stuck in your head.

House show—Also called *house concert.* An event, usually all ages, booked in someone's home or on their property. Traditionally a donation is asked for at the door and dinner is included, as well as a place to stay for traveling bands.

I

In the pocket—Slang for playing perfectly in tempo.

Input—The jack on an amp, instrument, pedal, or other device where you play an instrument in. *See also* Output.

Intro—The instrumental part at the beginning of a song, before the vocals come in.

Instrumentation—Which instruments are used in a particular song, as well as when and how they appear.

Instrument cable—*See* Cable.

Jack—A connecting device in an electrical component designed for the insertion of a plug. In simple terms, the hole in your guitar or amp that takes the plug end of a cord.

Jamming—Playing music informally with other people.

K

Key—The basic note or scale around which a song is organized.

Kit—Slang for *drum set.*

L

Levels—A term for the settings of volume and EQ on an instrument or piece of sound equipment such as a tape deck or PA.

Line-in—An electrical connection that allows an instrument or other sound source (not a mic) to go directly into a mixing console or other processing device.

Load-in—The process of carrying your gear from the van into the venue.

Local band—A band that lives in your town.

Lo-fi—*Low fidelity;* refers to sounds that have a less-polished DIY, or home-recorded, aesthetic. *See also* Hi-fi.

Lock in—To get in the pocket musically.

Loop—Recorded sounds played over and over.

Lyrics—The words to a song.

M

Mailing list—A list of people whom a band informs by e-mail or snail mail when they have a show.

Major label—A large company that pays for the recording, release, and distribution of music.

Manager—A person whose job is to help a band or performer with the business end of being a musician.

Measure—Also called *bar.* A unit of time (often four beats) expressed musically. *See also* Time signature.

Media contacts—Employees of magazines and newspapers who can be invited to shows, invited to write about a band, and to whom one might send a press kit.

Melody—The tune of a song.

Merch—Short for *merchandise,* a catch-all term for CDs, pins, T-shirts, zines, and other band-related wares.

Merch table—The place where bands can sell their CDs, pins, T-shirts, zines, and other band related wares. It gives audience members a mini store where they can buy stuff from their new favorite band.

Metronome—A time-keeping device used for reference by musicians to keep track of a beat while recording or playing live.

MIDI—*Musical Instrument Digital Interface;* a language allowing electronic instruments (such as keyboards) to communicate with a computer and each other to compose, arrange, and edit music.

Mix—The relative volume, panning, effects, and EQ of instruments in a recording or amplified at a live show.

Mixing console—Sometimes called a mixer soundboard, or just "board"; an audio device for combining, routing, and changing the tone, and/or panning of two or more signals.

Mono—Short for *monophonic*. A recording with only one channel. *See also* Stereo.

Moving units—Slang for selling things.

Multi-track—A term for recording technology that allows multiple channels to be recorded separately, one at a time or simultaneously.

Music scene—A group of people who play, appreciate, and support music of a particular genre, or in a particular location.

Music theory—The study of how music works, including the different elements comprising music, such as harmony, melody, rhythm, etc.

O

Off beat—Playing between beats; playing on the "and" of a count such as "1 and 2 and 3 and 4 and . . ."

Onboard effects—Effects built into an amp, instrument, or computer.

One—Often called "the one"; the first note of a measure.

One-four-five (I-IV-V) progression—A common chord progression using chords that are built upon the intervals of a fourth and a fifth above the tonic. An example of an I-IV-V progression is C-F-G.

Open mic—An event where performers sign up to play on a walk-in basis, with no booking necessary.

Opening band—An act who plays before the headliner.

Output—A connection jack that sends a signal (instrument or other sound) to another device.

Outro—The part of a song that is at the end, after the vocals are finished.

P

PA—Short for *public address* or *personal amplification* system; PA systems usually include mics, amps, soundboard, and speakers.

Pay-to-play—A scam that occurs when a slimy promoter sells bands bundles of tickets they have to sell in order to get paid.

Peaking—Reaching maximum amplitude (loudness); the term comes from the meters on the recorder that measure sound reaching their highest point. Beware of this as it can lead to distortion.

Pick—A small tool, usually plastic and often triangular, used for plucking the strings of stringed instruments played with the hands, such as guitar and bass.

Pitch—The level of sound in a scale in regard to is highness or lowness.

Playback—During recording, the playing of a track that has just been recorded.

Power amp—A device that supplies power to a pair of speakers.

Power strip—A device that contains several electrical outlets that can be plugged in to one wall outlet. Useful for supplying power to many appliances in a small space.

Pre-amp—Any electrical device that affects the signal going into an amp.

Presets—Tones or settings that come built in with some keyboards, amps, or other electronic devices.

Press kit—An informational packet about a band sent to the media. A press kit usually includes a photo, a bio, and sometimes a demo.

Press release—A short description of your event, as well as basic information about you or your band, which you can send to any news publication (print or online).

Progression—A sequence of chords.

Promoter—The person who is in charge of telling the whole world about the amazing upcoming show. Often the promoter and the booker are the same person. Promoting shows can include sending out a press release, hanging up fliers, and sending out online announcements.

Publicity—Getting the word out about your band.

Q

Quantize—A command used on a sampler when programming beats to correct rhythmic irregularities by moving notes to the nearest division of a beat.

¼-inch cord—Long cable (cord), also called an *instrument cable,* with a metal connecter about 1 inch long and ¼ inch in diameter at both ends, used to plug an instrument into an amp, PA, or effects box or to connect speakers.

R

R&B—Short for *rhythm and blues.*

Rack mounted—Sound-processing devices that are not built into the mixing console or the computer, but are screwed into a separate cabinet, or "rack."

Range—The distance between the lowest note and the highest note of an instrument or voice. Also used to discuss frequency when setting tones for instruments, amplifiers, and recording tools: *treble,* or high end, is a thinner, brighter, crisper or (at its extreme) brittle and shrill tone; *bass,* or the low end, adds warmth but can be muffling or boomy; and *mid* is just that, a combination of the two extremes but with some special qualities of its own.

Record label—A company that pays for the recording, release and distribution of sound recordings.

Register—The range or part of the range of a voice or instrument.

Rhythm—The timing, tempo, and beat of a piece of music.

Rhythm section—The part of a band responsible for keeping the rhythm going, usually drums and bass.

Riff—A short, repeated melodic or rhythmic phrase. Lots of rock songs are built entirely around riffs.

Rig—Slang for the *amp* or *amp-and-speaker combo* for guitars (bass rig, guitar rig).

Riot Grrrl—A feminist musical and social movement of the early '90s; associated with bands such as Bikini Kill, Bratmobile, and Huggy Bear.

Root note—Also called *the tonic,* this is the first note in the scale for any given chord (that is, C is the root note of the C chord); it is often the note that determines the key of a song.

S

Sample—A recorded digital copy of an audio signal.

Sampler—A device for making samples.

Scale—A succession of tones ascending or descending according to fixed intervals, in particular such a series beginning on a certain note, for example the major scale of C.

Sequencer—A device that records and remembers pattern information programmed into it.

Set—The duration of a band's or performer's time on stage. Also, the specific songs a band plays in its turn on stage and in what order.

Set list—The piece of paper (or napkin or flyer) that the band writes the order of the songs in its set on (one for each side of the stage and an extra for the drummer is nice).

The Settings—A catch-all term for the EQ, volume, and other controls over the sound quality of live or recorded music.

Sliding scale—A term for the practice of having an upper and lower limit for a ticket price. People then pay whatever they can afford in between the limits.

Snake—A thick, long cable holding multiple separate cables inside it that works like a big, long-distance extension cord for running cables from the stage to the PA. Every cord onstage plugs into a numbered input on the snake. The snake runs to the soundboard and plugs into the matching inputs on the board.

Solid state—Amplifier/sound processing technology that depends on circuit boards and electronics rather than tubes. *See also* Tube amp.

Solo—Playing alone; or the part of the song during which one instrument is featured.

Song structure—The order of the verse, chorus, and bridge.

Sound check—A mini rehearsal for a live show, wherein a band arrives at the venue early to set up their equipment on stage exactly as they will when they perform for an audience; everything is plugged in, including microphones and PA, and then each instrument and microphone and speaker is tested, alone and all together (if time allows) to make sure the sound system is working and that it all sounds good. Also a verb, to sound-check.

Soundperson—The person who works the soundboard in a live sound situation or a recording session. Also called a *sound engineer.*

Standard notation—Written musical notation using traditional notes, staffs, clefs, etc.

Standby switch—The switch on an amp or other tube-powered device that turns the speaker off but leaves the power on so that the tubes don't cool down. *See also* Tube amp.

Stereo—Two-channel sound, presented with a left and a right side. *See also* Mono.

Studio—A place where musicians record and/or rehearse.

Sync—To match up, or synchronize, one sound with another in time.

Syncopation—A style of playing that emphasizes the off beat. Playing so that emphasis is placed on the "and" of a "1 and 2 and 3 and four and" count.

Synthesizers—Electronic devices for making sounds and beats. Synthesizers often look like keyboards and contain preset tones and effects.

T

Tempo—The pace of the rhythm, usually referring to its specific beat and how fast or slow it is.

Time signature—A musical notation indicating the number of beats to a measure and the kind of note that takes a beat. Commonly this is expressed at the beginning of a song (either in the notation or just shared out loud between musicians) as a fraction in which the numerator is the number of beats per measure and the denominator represents the kind of note getting one beat.

Tour—A trip taken by musicians to get their music out into the world. When a band is on tour, they typically play shows almost every night, usually in a different town each night.

Transition—The movement in a song from one part to another.

Tube amp—An amplifier with vacuum tubes as apposed to transistors; known for warmth of tone.

12-inch—Shorthand for the diameter of a full-length vinyl record (LP), as opposed to a 7-inch (single) or 10-inch (EP).

U

Upstroke—An upward strum of hand, fingers, or pick over the strings of a guitar or similar instrument. *See also* Down stroke.

V

Venue—The place where a show is held.

Verse—The part of a musical song form (verse-chorus) that sets up the story or conveys a narrative. Is mainly in contrast to the chorus, which it leads into.

Volume—Another word for *loudness.*

Volume wars—A phenomenon where musicians keep turning their volumes up because they can't hear themselves and as a result, their sound keeps getting louder, drowning their bandmembers out, so that they have to turn up in order to hear themselves. No one wins a volume war.

X

XLR cord—A cord most often used to plug a microphone into a PA or mixer. An XLR cord has three prongs set in a triangle at one end and three holes in the same pattern at the other.

Z

Zine—A DIY/handmade publication, often used to spread the word about the writer's (the author of the zine) favorite indie bands. Also called fanzine.

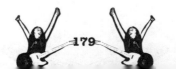

ROCK CAMPS

The Portland Rock Camp may be the first Rock Camp for Girls, but it's not the only one! Rock Camps are springing up all over the United States and in countries all over the world. The Girls Rock Camp Alliance (GRCA) is an organization formed to join together all the Girls Rock Camps in a concerted vision. Rock Camps that are part of the GRCA have adopted the following core values:

1. We value the power of music as a means to create personal and social change;
2. We value efforts that actively expand opportunities for girls and women;
3. We value positive approaches to fighting sexism;
4. We value integrity, honesty, and respect;
5. We value appropriate sharing of resources, cooperation, and collaboration;
6. We value using our collective voice to further our mission;
7. We value diversity.

To find out more about the Girls Rock Camp Alliance, go to Girlsrockcamp alliance.org.

Following is a list of Girls Rock Camp Alliance members as of 2007. Look for a camp near your home, or travel to a new place to go to Rock Camp!

Rock 'n' Roll Camp for Girls (Portland, OR)
www.girlsrockcamp.org
www.myspace.com/girlsrockcamp

Girls Rock NC (Durham, NC)
www.girlsrocknc.org

Southern Girls Rock & Roll Camp
(Murfreesboro, TN)
www.sgrrc.org

Popkollo (Hultsfred, Sweden)
www.popkollo.se/english
www.myspace.com/popkollo

Willie Mae Rock Camp for Girls (Brooklyn, NY)
www.williemaerockcamp.org
www.myspace.com/williemaerockcamp

Girls Rock! UK (London, England)
www.girlsrockuk.org
www.myspace.com/rocknrollcampforgirlsuk

Girls Rock Camp Austin (Austin, TX)
www.girlsrockcampaustin.org

Bay Area Girls Rock Camp (Oakland, CA)
www.bayareagirlsrockcamp.org
www.myspace.com/bayareagirlsrockcamp

Girlz Rhythm n Rock Camp (Columbus, OH)
www.girlzrhythmnrockcamp.com

Girls Rock! DC (Washington, D.C.)
www.girlsrockdc.org

Girls Rock Philly (Philadelphia, PA)
www.girlsrockphilly.org
www.myspace.com/girlsrockphilly

Girls Rock Camp ATL (Atlanta, GA)
www.girlsrockcampatl.org

Rock Camp for Girls Peterborough
(Peterborough, Ontario, Canada)
www.rc4gpeterborough.com

OTHER STUFF TO CHECK OUT

Girls Rock! The Movie, a documentary filmed at the Portland Rock 'n' Roll Camp for Girls in 2007, inspired Girls Rock! The Online Community. At the website, you'll find info about the movie, as well as a place to share music, ideas, and support with other like-minded women and girls. www.girlsrockmovie.com

The Punk Rock Aerobics fitness revolution starts in your mind. We aim to inspire, empower, and have a good time. Punk Rock Aerobics: The work out that rocks out.

"Punk Rock Aerobics" was put together with excerpts taken directly from the book *Punk Rock Aerobics: 75 Killer Moves, 50 Punk Classics, and 25 Reasons to Get Off Your Ass and Exercise*, by Maura Jasper and Hilken Mancini. Cambridge, MA: Da Capo Press, 2004. For more information about Punk Rock Aerobics, go to www.punkrockaerobics.com.

Vintage Synthesizers by Mark Vail. San Francisco: Miller Freeman Books, 2000.

Basic Chord Charts

The following charts will help you figure out what notes and chords you are playing on a guitar, bass, or keyboard. When you use them, keep a few things in mind:

1. Use all of your fingers, not just your pointer finger.
2. The circled letters on the guitar and bass charts mean that you can play that string open (that is, without pressing any fret).
3. Barré chords are played with your index finger pressing across all the strings and the rest of your fingers pressing the single notes on the frets.

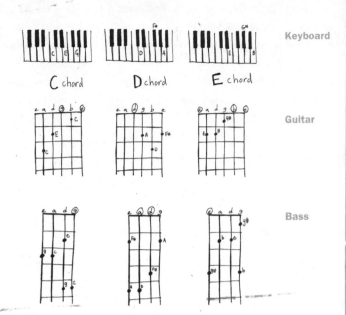

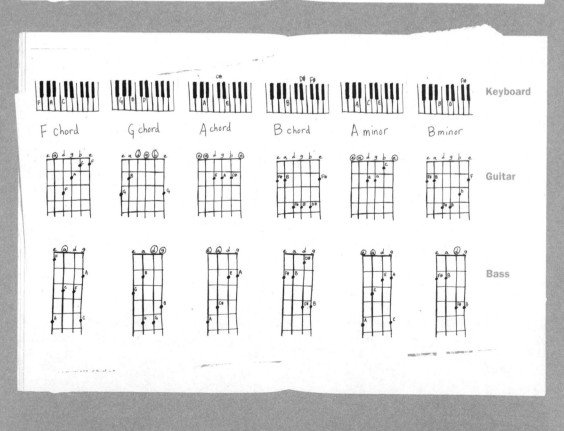

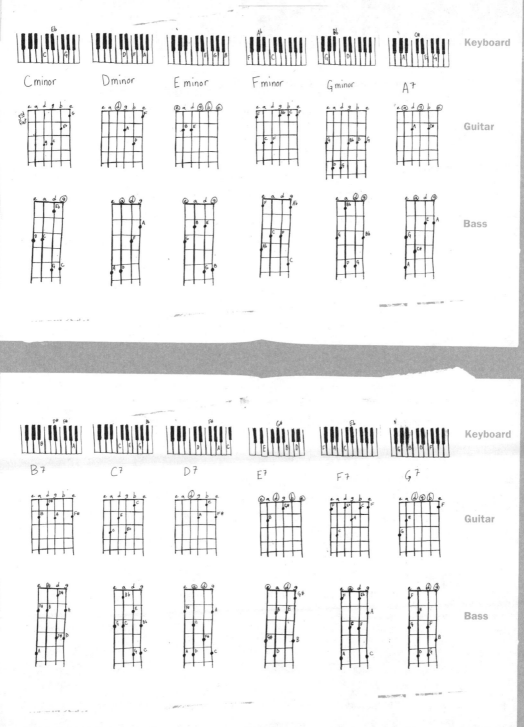

We MADE THis BOOK

 **AMANDA PAULK** learned most of what she knows about sound recording and amplification from working at her college radio station, WECI 91.5 FM in Richmond, Indiana; being on the student activities board at Earlham College; and trial and error. Though Amanda would never go so far as to call herself a musician, she had brief stints in the Harrodsburg High Marching Band and the Snatchclaws, and thinks making up songs with friends is really fun. Amanda believes anyone can understand and learn to run a simple sound system, no matter what the guys with ponytails and bad facial hair think.

 **AMY SABIN** took piano lessons briefly as a child but quickly quit due to lack of attention span (and the frustration of seeing a trampoline outside her teacher's window that she wasn't allowed to jump on). Her first keyboard was a six-inch-long Casio that played pop rock songs and lit up to show you how to play along. From that moment on she was hooked! Amy's past projects include drumming for the slips and the units, and playing keyboards for Krav Maga. She plays in an all-female rock band called the Phantom Lights, where she enjoys trading around with her bandmates on all the instruments.

 BECKY GEBHARDT was born and raised in Los Angeles, and she still lives there, too, when not touring with her band Raining Jane. She is self-taught on the bass and guitar and formally trained on the sitar, a twenty-string instrument from India. In 2005, Becky volunteered at a Rock 'n' Roll Camp for Girls summer session. She returned in 2007 along with the rest of Raining Jane.

 BETH DITTO was born to a wolf and a banshee under an amethyst sky in 1981, at the height of New Wave; unfortunately she was born in Arkansas, where Crystal Gayle and Billy Graham ruled the scene. She spent many days dancing to her own reflection in the TV glass, pretending to be the star of Wrigley's Spearmint gum commercials throughout the early '80s. In the late '90s, having survived the Arkansas wilderness, she and four friends found themselves in Olympia, Washington, sharing a two-bedroom house with six people and living off A&W hot dogs and root beer. Merely months later she was singing in a band called Gossip for fifteen kids and pizza crusts. Today she tours the world with the same band but has since moved out of the house and has a cat.

BETH WARSHAW-DUNCAN is a producer at WXPN-FM, a noncommercial radio station in Philadelphia, where she engineers live sessions with bands, directs live and recorded shows, and edits in soundproof studios all day (and all of the night). She is also certified as a teacher in Pennsylvania and runs a Writing for Radio class at the University of Pennsylvania, as well as workshops on production and sound-checking for the Black Lily Festival in Philadelphia. After volunteering for two years as a counselor and workshop instructor at the Willie Mae Rock Camp in New York, Beth founded and is the director of Girls Rock Philly (a founding member of the Girls Rock Camp Alliance), which held its first camp session in August 2007.

CAREY FAY-HOROWITZ has worked at the Rock 'n' Roll Camp for Girls for two seasons. She lives in Oakland, California, where she plays drums in a band called Songs for Moms. Carey is one of the founders of the Bay Area Girls Rock Camp, which opened in the summer of 2008.

John Clark

CARRIE BROWNSTEIN is a writer and musician. She was a member of the critically acclaimed rock band Sleater-Kinney. Her writing has appeared in the *New York Times,* the *Believer, Pitchfork,* and various book anthologies on music and culture. She co-wrote the Rock 'n' Roll Camp for Girls theme song and has been a volunteer at the camp since its inception. She lives in Portland, Oregon.

CHELSEY JOHNSON is a fiction writer, journalist, writing teacher, and graphic designer who lives in Portland, Oregon. At the Rock 'n' Roll Camp for Girls, she has been leading morning and afternoon assemblies since 2003. She co-wrote the camp theme song, and joined the board of directors in 2006. She also worked for Concordia Language Villages for nine years at their Norwegian language camps in Minnesota and Norway. Her writing has appeared in *Rolling Stone, Out, Chickfactor,* and *Ploughshares* and on NPR's *Selected Shorts.*

CLAUDIA LUCERO loves to make things, help people create spaces they love, and help Rock Camp find awesome volunteers. She's learning to play drums and belly dance, and she gets massages regularly as an amazing trade for Spanish lessons! She lives in sunny Portland, Oregon, with her honey and partner in crime, Jeff.

 **CONNIE WOHN** is a music industry multitasker and music maven. A self-employed music and hip-hop lover, all of her projects are ones that are close to her heart, from event production and marketing as creative director for the New York–based nonprofit World Up, an organization that works to connect the global communities of hip-hop, to booking and managing Portland's premier DJ collective, Stylus503. All of this experience led Connie to her position (among others) as marketing director for one of the City of Roses' biggest music festivals, Musicfest NW. But it is her teaching work and role as a publicist with the Rock 'n' Roll Camp for Girls, Willie Mae Rock Camp (NY), and Hip-Hop 101 at Jefferson High School that represent the culmination of years of experience and passion, combining her know-how as industry insider and music educator to enrich the lives of children through music.

 Poet, songwriter, and multi-instrumentalist **CYNTHIA NELSON** has released more than a dozen CDs of music over the years with her bands Ruby Falls, Retsin, and the Naysayer. A solo artist since 2001, her most recent work, *Homemade Map,* is available on an artist-owned media label, Nonstop Cooperative (www.nonstopco-op.com). She moved to Portland in 2005 after growing up in Northern California and living for fifteen years in New York City, Louisville, Kentucky, and on the road. She teaches guitar, bass, and drums and coaches bands at the Girls Rock Institute/Rock 'n' Roll Camp for Girls.

 **ELIZABETH VENABLE** has been playing guitar and a little bit of piano for the last fifteen years. Since joining the staff at Rock Camp, she's also become literate with the drums and bass. Her first band was a guitar duo called Weary Gentleman's Saloon, founded when she was sixteen. Since then she's played in several other bands, including Papa M, and the Naysayer with Cynthia Nelson. She also writes and performs her own songs as Venable. Elizabeth lives in Portland, Oregon, where she teaches at the Rock 'n' Roll Camp for Girls, drives a taxi cab, and works on art and music.

 **EMMA MCKENNA** lives in Toronto, Canada. She has been teaching at the Rock 'n' Roll Camp for Girls in Portland since the summer of 2004. Emma was a guitarist/vocalist in the lesbian rock band Galaxy for a three-year stint. When Galaxy broke up in the spring of 2007, Emma did what she had to do: Write songs for one person to play and one to sing. She is teaching herself the drums and just put out her own EP. Emma spends her days studying feminist and queer theory and her nights wearing earplugs.

FAY FUNK is a senior at Wilson High School in Portland, Oregon. She has been playing bass guitar for three years.

 **HILKEN MANCINI** is a singer/guitarist and dancer. She studied at the Boston Conservatory before forming the band Fuzzy (Atlantic Records), which she co-fronted. She is co-creator of Punk Rock Aerobics (PRA) with Maura Jasper, and currently plays music in the band Shepherdess (www. shepherdessband.com). She became a certified aerobics instructor with the AFAA for the very first PRA class, held in Boston in August 2001. She currently plays an SG Junior and an electric blue Cort Flying V.

 A product of suburban Washington DC, **JODI DARBY** was first radicalized in the Reagan-era 1980s, when she was absorbed into the political-punk world of Positive Force DC and became involved in antiwar and anticapitalist organizing. She has been involved in self-defense training and instruction for the past twelve years, working with Seattle's Home Alive and Womenstrength in Portland, Oregon, as well as the Rock 'n' Roll Camp for Girls. A self-proclaimed mediaphile, she produces a twice-monthly radio program with the Circle A Radio collective on KBOO 90.7 FM, which addresses current feminist and antiauthoritarian movements. She lives and works in Portland, where she teaches Multi-Media Arts at Portland YouthBuilders, an alternative high school for underserved youth. She enjoys strong coffee and long walks on the beach.

 **KARLA SCHICKELE** is a musician and songwriter, and plays in the bands Ida and K. Her previous projects include Beekeeper, the Naysayer, and Ducks on the Pond. She runs around with a clipboard at the Willie Mae Rock Camp for Girls in New York City, and sometimes gets to teach bass and lead songwriting workshops, too.

 **KAIA WILSON** has been playing and writing music since she was a wee tiny one. Over the last sixteen years, she has played in three bands (Adickdid, Team Dresch, the Butchies) and maintained a solo career, touring all the while. She has collaborated with Amy Ray (Indigo Girls) on her solo projects, and started and ran a record label, Mr. Lady Records (1997–2003), with then partner Tammy Rae Carland. When she's not busy rocking out or getting mellow on the acoustic, Kaia likes to spend her time running around like a maniac along the banks of the Sandy River in Portland, Oregon, with her dogs Andy(snack)

and Basket(ball). (She also loves her two kitties and spends endless hours playing with them with the bird-on-a-stick toy.) Her other life passions involve anything with animals, especially sea turtles, landscaping involving natural stone, and perfecting her salsa recipes.

KATE WALSH has worked with the Rock 'n' Roll Camp for Girls for over three years; she is also a founding member of the Girls Rock Camp Alliance. She plays keys, saxophone, and guitar and loves music theory. She graduated with a degree in Rocking Out Studies from New York University, and is studying Youth Arts and Community Development at Columbia College Chicago while playing and recording with her bands Speck Mountain and Pocket Parade. In her spare time, Kate enjoys bikes, 16-inch softball, reading, and Boggle.

KATELYN MUNDAL is half Norwegian and half American. She was born in Seattle in 1989 and moved to Norway when she was four, where she has lived pretty much ever since. She started playing guitar when she was fourteen and drums when she was sixteen. The first band she ever played in was Spirit Fruit Jam at Camp during the summer of 2006. Since then she has played in a few short-lived bands with friends, but nothing very serious. She finds herself happy just sitting in her room strumming out the odd chord on the guitar or jamming with her brother.

Currently serving as artistic director of the Rock 'n' Roll Camp for Girls, **MARISA ANDERSON** came to Rock Camp as a volunteer in 2004. She currently performs with the Evolutionary Jass Band and as a solo artist. She has recorded six albums, toured nationally and internationally, and had her music placed in several film and television soundtracks. Previous projects include the Dolly Ranchers and the One Railroad Circus.

MAURA JASPER is a conceptual mulitmedia artist whose work investigates how pop cultures and histories shape and inform identity. She has exhibited and screened work widely in the United States and overseas, including Artist's Space, Threadwaxing Space, the Institue of Contemporary Art in Boston, and the Centre for Contemporary Images in Geneva. She is probably best known as co-founder of Punk Rock Aerobics, the DIY workout.

MIRAH YOM TOV ZEITLYN is a singer and a writer of songs. Most of her seven albums have been released on the K record label. She is a proud supporter of the Rock 'n' Roll Camp for Girls. Now living in Portland, Oregon, Mirah divides her time between national and international touring, working on her next solo album, occasional moonlighting in a Stevie Nicks cover band, and spending quality time at home with her garden and girlfriend.

MIREAYA MEDINA is a singer-songwriter and experimental keyboardist who was born and raised in Portland, Oregon. She began singing at the age of nine in her school chorus and at twelve received her first Casio keyboard. This was the foundation of her passion for writing music. In 2004, she started a duo called Escape from Keyboard Island, which focused on nontraditional combinations of instruments such as keyboards, accordion, beat machine, and vocals. She dubbed the unique sound of Escape from Keyboard Island as *lo-tech-carni-synth-ho* with somewhat of a goth influence. In Mireaya's solo project, Cheetah Finess, she uses beat machines, samplers, synthesizers, and vocals. Cheetah Finess's sound is based on hip-hop, soul, and electronic musical roots and has an experimental, driven, dance quality. She is recording and producing, and hopes to eventually release some great new music to dance to.

NATHAN KENNEY has played guitar for about seven years, most recently in the apathetically strange Portland band Special Guest. After hearing about Rock Camp during a 2004 Sleater-Kinney show, Nathan joined up to handle gear and any other miscellaneous odd jobs that needed doing. Interesting facts: Campers are fascinated with his sideburns, and he does a wicked impression of the "DJ" keyboard.

NAZMIA JAMAL was born in 1979 of East African Asian descent and grew up in South Wales. She has been writing zines for over a decade, most recently the "collective experience" zine *The Tea and Sympathy Postal Network*. In 2001 she became involved in organizing Ladyfest London, the second Ladyfest to take place in the United Kingdom. Since then she has been a regular organizer of queer and feminist events both on her own and with the Bakery Ladies collective. In 2006, Nazmia volunteered at the Rock 'n' Roll Camp for Girls in Portland and subsequently began planning for a similar camp in the U.K. Girls Rock! UK hosted its first Ladies Rock! camp in August 2007. Nazmia has been a volunteer youth worker at local women's and LGBT youth groups, and runs workshops in various crafts. She has lived in London since 1997, where she teaches English at a comprehensive sixth form and is studying for an MA in Gender, Sexuality, Politics and Culture.

Illustrator **NICOLE J. GEORGES** is also a zinester from Portland, Oregon. She publishes an autobiographical comic zine called *Invincible Summer,* and paints pet portraits of lucky animals. Nicole likes to sing and play the keyboard, and has done so in the bands the Sour Grapes and ?Fact or Fiction. She has been affiliated with the Rock Camp since 2001, and never gets tired of seeing ladies and girls rock and write at zine workshops. Visit her at www.nicolejgeorges.com.

 **SARAH DOUGHER** has been playing and writing about rock for over fifteen years. She plays guitar, bass, and organ and has made eight records in a musical career that started in Austin, Texas, where she played with Molly Gove in the band Veronica. She moved back to her home state of Oregon in 1995, and played with sts in a band called the Lookers. Then they started playing with Corin Tucker (of Sleater-Kinney) in Cadallaca. Dougher also played under her own name with Jon Rueter and other members, touring internationally. Now she writes music for singers and plays in a band called the SGs, with Sarah Gottesdiener and Steve Gevurtz. She teaches a class about the history of women in rock at Portland State University, and teaches music in downtown Portland.

 SHANNON O'BRIEN has been involved with the Rock 'n' Roll Camp for Girls as a student, intern, volunteer, and instructor since the fall of 2005. She plays bass and has been in several bands including pinion, the Revenents, and On Y Va. Currently, she is looking to make noise in Olympia, Washington.

 Photographer **SHAYLA HASON** is a musician based in Portland, Oregon. Her work has appeared in *ANP Quarterly; O, The Oprah Magazine;* and the *Vice* photo issue, among others. Addicted to reading, she nevertheless credits music with saving her life during adolescence. Her work can be seen at www.dokuchan.com.